Cambridge First Certificate in English 3

Cambridge
First Certificate
in English
3

Examination papers from the University of Cambridge Local Examinations Syndicate

CAMBRIDGE
UNIVERSITY PRESS

PUBLISHED BY THE PRESS SYNDICATE OF THE UNIVERSITY OF CAMBRIDGE
The Pitt Building, Trumpington Street, Cambridge CB2 1RP, United Kingdom

CAMBRIDGE UNIVERSITY PRESS
The Edinburgh Building, Cambridge CB2 2RU, United Kingdom
40 West 20th Street, New York, NY 1011–4211, USA
10 Stamford Road, Oakleigh, Melbourne 3166, Australia

First published 1997
Reprinted 1997

Printed in the United Kingdom at the University Press, Cambridge

ISBN 0 521 58726 3 Student's Book
ISBN 0 521 58725 5 Teacher's Book
ISBN 0 521 58724 7 Set of 2 Cassettes

Contents

Thanks and acknowledgements

The tests in the Student's Book were specially written by UCLES item writers who have prepared the materials strictly according to the 1996 FCE Specifications: Angela ffrench, Mark Harrison, Nick Kenny, Suzanne Lawson, Jackie Martin, Brian Orpet, Amos Paran, Tim Potter and Katy Salisbury. We are also grateful to Annette Capel and Jean Lister for their work on Paper 2 and Alison Silver and Paul Henderson for their work on Paper 1 and Paper 4. The Student's Book and Teacher's Book were edited by Vanessa Jakeman with the assistance of Subject Officers and staff in the EFL Division at UCLES.

The publishers are grateful to the following for permission to reproduce copyright material. It has not always been possible to identify sources of all the material used, and in such cases the publishers would welcome information from the copyright owners.

Girl About Town for the texts on pp. 5, 6 and 63-64; *The Independent* for the texts on pp. 8, 11-12, 34-35, 58 and 69-70 by Keith Elliott, Stella Yarrow, Stuart Rising, Martin Kelner and Brian Cathcart; Secker & Warburg for the text on pp. 17-18 from *Made in America* by Bill Bryson. Copyright © 1994 Bill Bryson. Reproduced by permission of Greene & Heaton Ltd; *Unique* for the text on p. 19; Aspen Specialist Media for the texts on pp. 23 and 71. Reproduced courtesy of *Active Life* magazine, November/December 1995 issue; *The Guardian* for the texts on pp. 31, 84-85 and 95. © The Guardian; HarperCollins Publishers and Penguin USA for the text on p. 32 from *A zoo in my luggage* by Gerald Durrell; *Q Magazine* for the text on pp. 37-38 by Mike Burwood; *The New Scientist* for the text on p. 43; The BBC for the extract from the BBC Radio 4 programme *You and Yours* on which the listening exercise on p. 54 is based and for the BBC Radio Cambridgeshire extract on which the listening exercise on p. 104 is based; Nicki Pope/*Marie Claire*/Robert Harding Syndication for the text on pp. 56-57 by Nicola Walters from *Marie Claire*; *The Times* for the text on pp. 60-61 by Lucy Gribble, © Lucy Gribble /*The Times*, 26th June 1995 and the text on p. 75 by John Goodbody, © Times Newspapers Limited, 1995; Caroline Sanders for the text on p. 83 from *Outlook*; *The European* for the texts on pp. 86-87 and 89-90; Sheldon Press for the text on p. 97 from *Body Language*.

Text permissions by Sophie Dukan.

Photographs (black and white): Adam Scott for p. 8; Janine Wiedel for pp. 11, 37 and 60; Tony Stone Images/Alan Smith for p. 34; Sylvia Cordaiy/Jonathan Smith for p. 64; Ian Took/Biofotos for p. 86; Barnaby's Picture Library/Philip Little for p. 89. Picture research by Sandie Huskinson-Rolfe (PHOTOSEEKERS)

Drawings pp. 39, 65 by Julian Page

Colour section: The Image Bank for photographs 1E (top and centre) and 2C. All other photographs are reproduced courtesy of UCLES. Artwork by Angela ffrench/Gecko Ltd.

Book design by Peter Ducker MSTD

Cover design by Dunne & Scully

The cassettes which accompany this book were recorded at Studio AVP, London.

To *the student*

This book is for candidates preparing for the University of Cambridge Local Examinations Syndicate (UCLES) First Certificate in English examination (FCE). It contains four complete tests which you can practise on your own or with the help of your English teacher. The tests are based on the revised FCE syllabus introduced in December 1996.

The FCE examination is part of a group of examinations developed by UCLES called the Cambridge Main Suite. The Main Suite consists of five examinations that have similar characteristics but are designed for different levels of English language ability. Within the five levels, FCE is at Cambridge Level 3.

| Cambridge Level 5
Certificate of Proficiency in English (CPE) |
| Cambridge Level 4
Certificate in Advanced English (CAE) |
| **Cambridge Level 3**
First Certificate in English (FCE) |
| Cambridge Level 2
Preliminary English Test (PET) |
| Cambridge Level 1
Key English Test (KET) |

The FCE examination consists of five papers:
Paper 1 – a **Reading** paper of 1 hour 15 minutes
Paper 2 – a **Writing** paper of 1 hour 30 minutes
Paper 3 – a **Use of English** paper of 1 hour 15 minutes
Paper 4 – a **Listening** paper of about 40 minutes
Paper 5 – a **Speaking** paper of about 14 minutes

Paper 1   Reading
This paper consists of **four parts**. Each part contains a text and some questions. Part 4 may contain two or more shorter related texts. There are **thirty-five questions** in total, including multiple choice, gapped text and matching.

Paper 2   Writing
This paper consists of **two parts**. Part 1 is **compulsory**. It provides texts and visual material to help you write a letter of 120–180 words.

In Part 2, there are four tasks from which you **choose one** to write about. The range of tasks from which questions may be drawn includes an article, a report, a composition, a short story and a letter. The last question is based on the set books. These books remain on the list for about two years and you should contact UCLES or the UCLES local secretary in your area, if you wish to have the up-to-date list of background reading texts. If you decide to do the question on the set books, there will be two options from which you can choose **one** to write about. You have to write 120–180 words.

Paper 3   Use of English
This paper contains exercises of various kinds which test your control of English grammar, vocabulary and spelling. There are **five parts** and **sixty-five questions** in this paper.

Paper 4   Listening
This paper contains **four parts**. Each part contains a recorded text or texts and some questions including multiple choice, note-taking and matching. You hear each text twice. There is a total of **thirty questions**.

Paper 5   Speaking
This paper consists of **four parts**. The standard test format is two candidates and two examiners. One examiner takes part in the conversation, the other examiner just listens. You will be given photographs and other visual material to look at and talk about. Sometimes you will talk with the other candidate, sometimes with the examiner and sometimes with both.

Marks and results

The five FCE papers total 200 marks, after weighting. Each paper is weighted to 40 marks. Your overall FCE grade is based on the total score gained in all five papers. It is not necessary to achieve a satisfactory level in all five papers in order to pass the examination. Certificates are given to candidates who pass the examination with grade A, B or C. A is the highest. The minimum successful performance in order to achieve a Grade C corresponds to about 60% of the total marks. You will also be informed if you do particularly well in any individual paper. D, E and U (unclassified) are failing grades. If you fail you will be informed about the papers in which your performance was particularly weak.

The FCE examination is widely recognised in commerce and industry and in individual university faculties and other educational institutions.

Further information

For more information about FCE, or any other UCLES examination write to:

EFL Division
UCLES
1 Hills Road
Cambridge
CB1 2EU
England

Tel: +44 1223 553311
Fax: +44 1223 460278

Test 1

PAPER 1 READING (1 hour 15 minutes)

Part 1

You are going to read an article about fashion shows. Choose the most suitable heading from the list **A–I** for each part (**1–7**) of the article. There is one extra heading which you do not need to use. There is an example at the beginning (**0**).
Mark your answers **on the separate answer sheet**.

A	Having new ideas
B	Keeping things under control
C	Making the clothes
D	Who's going to wear the clothes?
E	Disappointments to overcome
F	Everything depends on the show
G	Making it all look attractive
H	It's worth all the stress
I	No time off for designers

Fashion shows

Putting on a fashion show is not as glamorous as it looks – Sharon Stansfield finds out what the stress is all about.

| **0** | *I* |

The shows – Milan, London and Paris – are over for another season. Fashion journalists can put down their notebooks with a sigh of relief, and buyers can return to their offices. For the designers, there is hardly time to congratulate themselves or lick their wounds before the whole business starts all over again. In just four months they must have their next collection of clothes ready for the March shows.

| **1** | |

Over the next few months, designers and their creative teams will work together to create a spectacle that will hopefully fire the imagination of the fashion journalists and wake up the buyers. If the show's a failure and no-one wants to buy, the designer could be out of work. There's more than models' bad moods to worry about – show-time is nerve-racking for everyone involved, from the designers to the wardrobe people.

| **2** | |

Designer Paul Frith describes the nightmare of working on a show. 'It can be pure madness backstage. That's the only time I ever wonder why I'm doing it. It just becomes chaos. There's just so much to think about. I spend the whole time in a state of high anxiety. But when it's finished, I just can't wait for the next one. The shows are the reason I do what I do and I get a real thrill out of them.'

| **3** | |

Paul Frith's last collection was well received. But after taking a short break, it was not long before he began to think about his next collection. Designers work a year ahead, so right now they'll be working on collections that will be in the shops this time next year. However, inspiration is not a thing that can be turned on and off whenever you like, and though designers work to tight schedules, Paul Frith explains how creativity can't be timetabled to suit. 'All of a sudden I get this feeling in my head, then I sit down and sketch and it just pours out of me.'

| **4** | |

Once the designs are on paper and the designer has chosen the fabrics he or she wants to work with, the sample collection for the shows can be produced. This is carried out by the design team under the designer's supervision. Firstly, the cutter makes an initial pattern of the garment from the designer's sketch. Then a model is made, which is then altered by the designer until it is exactly how they want it. Finally, the perfected patterns are passed over to a machinist.

| **5** | |

While the garments are being made, the designer starts to work with a stylist. Together they decide on how the collection is going to be presented at the shows. This involves deciding what hats, bags, belts, etc. should be used, and the hiring of the creative team – choreographer, producer, hair-stylist and make-up artist. The more money a designer has available, the more experts he or she can employ to create a successful show.

| **6** | |

About a month before the show is due to take place, the stylist will begin to visit modelling agencies. Getting models with the right look is extremely difficult if the budget is tight. Fashion shows have a reputation for being badly paid, and often models chosen for a show will drop out at the last moment if they get a better paid job, like an advert. However, a show that gets a lot of press coverage can make a new model's name.

| **7** | |

When things aren't certain even up to the last minute, it's no wonder there's an atmosphere of panic backstage. While the designer may be wondering why he or she didn't take up painting instead of fashion, it is up to the stylist to remain calm and in command. As head of the creative team, the stylist must make sure that everyone knows exactly what they're doing. There is only one run-through before the real thing and this is when the stylist has to get everyone organised. Whether the show is a triumph or a disaster depends on that.

Part 2

You are going to read an article by a journalist who took a residential course for writers.
For Questions **8–14**, choose the answer (**A, B, C** or **D**) which you think fits best according
to the text.
Mark your answers **on the separate answer sheet**.

ON Monday, 14th November, it rained all day. 'Is this a bad sign?' I wondered as I asked a local person for directions to the venue for my course. As I was late, I was glad his instructions were brief and clear, but I thought he had a strange expression on his face. 'Danger of flooding. Check your brakes,' read the next sign. The sign after that read 'Arvon Foundation', where my course was. It also said 'Drive carefully.' I edged towards my destination. It was too late to turn back.

When I'd mentioned that I was going on a writing course my friends' reactions had varied from 'Are you running it?' to 'You must be mad.' The latter was right, I thought, as I walked into a 16th century farmhouse just before dinner. I was shown to a small room with three beds and a wash basin. The only bathroom was through another bedroom. For a journalist with wide experience of 5-star hotels, this was a shock.

I took my place at the dinner table and looked at my companions for the next five days; sixteen would-be fiction writers, aged 26–74. We had two teachers: Deborah, author of ten novels, and Stephen, whose latest work I had been unable to find in one of the biggest bookshops in London. 'Hi, I'm Stephen,' he said amiably, sitting down next to me. Without thinking, I confessed to my failure in the bookshop, which added to the strain of the occasion for us both.

After dinner, our course in fiction writing began. 'What do you want to get out of your course here?' Stephen enquired, and we each explained our plans. Mine had been a novel. When I'd booked the course, I'd left lots of free time to plot it out, identify the characters and write at least one chapter. But all this time was swallowed up by less demanding activities, like going to parties. 'Er, a short story …' I heard myself saying weakly, but at least it sounded like something I could achieve.

It seemed less so the next day, when I was faced with the blank screen on the word processor I had brought with me. There was nothing between me and my fiction but writer's block. But professional journalists like me don't get writer's block, do they? Wrong. Fortunately, no-one else could get started either.

Towards the end of the morning, I remembered that I had an ancient piece of fiction in my machine. This was a desperate idea but I had to have something to show the teachers before the afternoon's individual tutorials. Perhaps it could be turned into a short story. It didn't take more than a quick glance at it to convince me that it could.

Then it was tutorial time. We were due for our 20-minute individual session and nerves were frayed by the threat of cruel assessment. We had heard of idle tutors who refused to read the students' work at all and of frank ones who dared to tell the truth about it, but we were much luckier. Deborah and Stephen were thorough in their preparation. Stephen provided detailed analysis from handwritten notes; Deborah supplied brilliant solutions to tricky problems; both were heartwarmingly encouraging to everyone.

By Thursday evening, the brave were reading their own stories, which provided fascinating insights into their lives and personalities. Predictably, standards varied from the truly talented to the deeply ungifted, but all were clapped and praised, as they deserved to be. Most of the stories were autobiographical – so how come mine, which I was too cowardly to read – was about a world I know nothing about? And how come I got the distinct impression that Deborah and Stephen thought I'd better stick to journalism?

8 How did the writer feel as she made her way to the course?

   A confused

   B annoyed

   C nervous

   D determined

9 When the writer arrived for the course, she

   A felt that some of her friends' reactions had been right.

   B was disappointed that the building was such an old one.

   C considered complaining about the lack of facilities.

   D suspected that it was likely to be badly run.

10 In line 30 'my failure' refers to the fact that the writer

   A didn't remember Stephen from the bookshop.

   B hadn't found Stephen's new book.

   C didn't realise Stephen worked with Deborah.

   D couldn't start a conversation with Stephen.

11 Before she went on the course, the writer had

   A managed to write a short story to take with her.

   B decided that writing a novel was going to take too long.

   C not had as much free time as she'd expected.

   D not succeeded in putting her plans into action.

12 What happened when she sat down to write on the first morning?

   A She discovered that she could have the same problems as any other writer.

   B She realised that something she had written in the past was excellent.

   C She overcame a problem with the machine she had taken with her.

   D She decided that her first idea for a story was unlikely to work.

13 What does the writer say about the first tutorial?

   A The teachers didn't tell them what they really thought of their work.

   B It was better than those given on some other courses for writers.

   C She was more nervous about it than some of the other writers.

   D She thought that Stephen's approach wasn't as useful as Deborah's.

14 When people read their own stories to the others,

   A different stories got different reactions.

   B there was no opportunity for the writer to read hers.

   C the stories revealed things about their writers.

   D the writer felt that they were better than hers.

Part 3

You are going to read a newspaper article about a schoolboy race walker. Eight sentences have been removed from the article. Choose from the sentences **A–I** the one which fits each gap (**15–21**). There is one extra sentence which you do not need to use. There is an example at the beginning (**0**).

Mark your answers **on the separate answer sheet**.

A schoolboy with the world at his feet

STUART MONK'S mates hate walking to school with him. It's only 10 minutes from the 16-year-old's home, even for those going slowly because they can't face a maths lesson. Others, happy that they have done their homework, will probably take half that time. | **0** | *I* |

'Everybody keeps telling me to slow down when I'm walking with them,' he admits. | **15** | He happens to be Britain's brightest star in the unglamorous sport of race walking.

At the national junior championships in two weeks' time, he will be trying for a sub-45 minute time in the 10km walk to qualify for the European Championships. | **16** | 'But his times have been 58, 54, 50 and 46 minutes,' says his trainer, Pauline Wilson proudly. 'And in the last race he had an injury which slowed him up a bit.'

Race walking is a strange sport. People laugh at it because of the number of walkers who are disqualified during races. With no technology to help them, judges have to decide whether the rules are being broken because a walker has failed to keep contact with the ground. Since walkers are going so fast, it's hard for them to do so accurately. Every top walker has been disqualified from a race at one time or another. | **17** | It's so common that under the rules you are warned twice before being thrown out of a race.

Race walking hasn't been very good at responding to bad publicity, even though it's got a very strong argument purely on health grounds. It is the perfect form of exercise, using all the large muscles, and it causes very few injuries, even if you're moving along as fast as the average cyclist. It's also a wonderfully cheap sport. **18** [   ] His only income comes from delivering newspapers.

Stuart is already part of his regional senior team and set a UK under-20 record when he won the national Indoor Championships in February. He is in the middle of school exams but still found time to compete in a local race. Before I went to meet him there I asked Pauline Wilson how I would recognise him. 'Don't worry. **19** [   ]', she replied. And he was.

Pauline is in no doubt about Stuart's potential. 'It's very exciting to see him improve,' she says. He is certainly capable of being part of the Olympic team one day. To reach that level, it takes a lot of effort. **20** [   ] But he's only 16, so it's really too early to say.'

21 [   ] Stuart himself finds it hard to explain, though Pauline thinks that it's a combination of physical advantages, self-discipline and maturity. 'I'm aware of what it takes to reach the top,' says Stuart. It's a long walk, but he's getting there.

A Even Stuart, in his short career, has had this happen to him twice.

B This makes it just right for a 16-year-old like Stuart.

C Stuart is determined to win one, though.

D What is the special talent that makes Stuart walk faster than most people can run?

E That would be quite an achievement for someone who only took up the sport seriously 12 months ago.

F Stuart has the right mental attitude and the right discipline.

G However, that isn't easy for Stuart.

H Stuart will be the one in the lead.

I But Stuart can walk the distance faster than most people could cycle it.

Part 4

You are going to read a magazine article about companies which develop photographs. For Questions **22–35**, choose from the companies (**A–E**). Some of the companies may be chosen more than once. When more than one answer is required, these may be given in any order. There is an example at the beginning (**0**). Mark your answers **on the separate answer sheet**.

Of which company or companies are the following stated?

It takes a day for the prints to be returned to the shop.	**0**	*A*	
It offers services at different prices.	**22**		
The writer had chosen a good day on which to use it.	**23**		
It failed to do anything within the period it guaranteed.	**24**		
Everything about the packaging was fine.	**25**		**26**
The photos were accompanied by advertising material.	**27**		
The writer was confused about what to do.	**28**		
There was no protection for the negatives.	**29**		
The writer's experience of it was better than that of later customers.	**30**		
It lets you choose whether to be sent advertising material or not.	**31**		
The writer used it because another service was not available.	**32**		

Its methods appear more scientific than another company's.

33	

Other people could see the photos being developed.

34	

It may give customers their money back.

35	

Photograph Developers

When having your precious holiday photographs developed, how much difference is there between companies? STELLA YARROW tested five of them.

Films Plus   A

This wasn't my first choice. I'd intended to try out another company first, but the machinery in the branch I visited was being replaced (the shop had neglected to tell me this when I rang the day before). The service at *Films Plus*, in keeping with its low-cost image, is of the Do-It-Yourself variety. Customers fill in details on an envelope and deposit their films in a container. After laboriously completing the form (having had some difficulty understanding the prices and instructions), I realised the films are picked up only once a week, on Thursday, for returning on the Friday. Luckily, this was a Wednesday. But even if I'd waited longer, it's hard to complain at this price.

Packaging: Flimsy, and the strips of negatives were all in one sleeve, not separate ones as they should have been. ⟫➜

Quickprint | B

The film was processed in the shop's own mini-laboratory, where technicians in white coats operated mysterious-looking machinery. The prints were ready within the hour, as guaranteed, and there was nothing to criticise in the service. I was lucky, though: my pictures were the last to be developed before they ran out of paper and the service was halted, to the annoyance of a queue of customers. The service is cheaper if you are prepared to wait longer for your pictures.
Packaging: Reasonably strong and the negatives were properly sleeved.

Photo Express | C

I went to the branch of this chain of mini-laboratories based in a local chemist's shop. The set-up looked less laboratory-like than *Quickprint*, with the machinery turning out lines of strangers' family snapshots in view of customers buying medicines or shampoo. The snaps were ready within the hour, as advertised, and cheaper than *Quickprint*.
Packaging: The negatives were in a separate bag in separate sleeves and they and the photos were in a strong envelope made of card.

Snapshots | D

The prints from this mail-order company were slightly better than those of its competitor,

Pictureland, but it trailed behind on service. It promised that the mail-order envelopes I requested would arrive within three days; they took five. A second batch I asked for when the first lot didn't turn up took a week. The prints were returned to me ten days after the film was posted to the company, although the company says prints are returned within seven to nine days of posting. At such a rock-bottom price, the company doesn't throw in a free film – but I was sent a mass of leaflets for more expensive sister companies, which do.
Packaging: Flimsy, but the negatives were satisfactorily packed.

Pictureland | E

The mail-order envelopes I asked for turned up a day later than promised, but the service was otherwise efficient. The company guarantees you a refund if it doesn't get the snaps back to you within seven days. It met this target, just – they took seven days to get to me. *Snapshots* on the other hand, didn't offer such a guarantee and took longer. One fault with *Pictureland* is that you must ring a special number if you don't want to be flooded with brochures and leaflets in future.
Packaging: The negatives were lying loose in the envelope and could easily have been badly damaged.

PAPER 2   WRITING (1 hour 30 minutes)

Part 1

You **must** answer this question.

1   You have decided to have a party to celebrate your birthday. You found an advertisement for Big Sounds Disco and decide to ask for further information.

Read carefully the advertisement and the notes you have made. Then, using this information, write a letter to David Price, the man who runs the disco. You should cover all the points in your notes. You may add relevant information of your own.

BIG SOUNDS DISCO

Music/Entertainment/Fun

for all occasions:
weddings, parties

Book now for the summer season

Music from the
50s, 60s, 70s, 80s, 90s

(All kinds) Rock Pop, Jazz, etc.

DAVID PRICE

9th July, 8.30 – 12.00 – okay?

Ambrose Hotel – large private room booked

About 40 people

Cost?

Competitions for dancing?

Say what I want

Write **a letter** of between **120** and **180** words in an appropriate style on the next page. Do not write any addresses.

Part 1

Part 2

Write an answer to **one** of the questions **2–5** in this part. Write your answers in **120–180** words in an appropriate style on the next page. Put the question number in the box.

2   A group of English-speaking students is going to study at your college for three months and they have asked for different kinds of information. You have been given the task of writing a report for them on **the shops** in your area.

  Write your **report,** giving some details about such things as types of shops and opening times, and making recommendations on suitable places for students to spend their money.

3   You are on holiday for two weeks with a group of people whom you have not met before but who share the same interests as you. At the end of your first week, you decide to write a letter to your pen friend, telling him/her about the group, your activities so far and what you plan to do during your second week.

  Write your **letter**.

4   Your class has recently had a discussion on violence on television and in films today. Your teacher has now asked you to write a composition giving your opinion on the following statement.

  Violence on television and in films can make young people behave badly.

  Write your **composition**.

5   **Background reading texts**

  Answer **one** of the following two questions based on your reading of **one** of the set books.

  (a) Choose two places described in the book or in any of the short stories you have read. Write a **composition**, explaining why they are important to the book or short stories.

  (b) You have agreed to write an article for the college magazine on the book which you have read. You should write about the development of the story, giving examples of where the story is easy to follow and where it is more complicated. Write your **article**.

Part 2

Question	

PAPER 3   USE OF ENGLISH (1 hour 15 minutes)

Part 1

For Questions **1–15**, read the text below and decide which answer, **A**, **B**, **C** or **D** best fits each space. There is an example at the beginning (**0**).
Mark your answers **on the separate answer sheet**.

Example:

0   **A** took   **B** went   **C** became   **D** made

0	A	B	C	D
	—	—	▬	—

THE TELEPHONE IN THE US

The telephone was invented in 1876 by Alexander Graham Bell, a Scotsman who **(0)** .... a US citizen. The word 'telephone' had been **(1)** .... existence since the 1830s and had been **(2)** .... to a number of inventions designed to produce sound.

Bell had become interested in the possibility of long-distance speech **(3)** .... his work with the deaf. He was twenty-eight and his assistant, Thomas Watson, was **(4)** .... twenty-one when they **(5)** .... their great success on 10th March 1876. Despite their long and **(6)** .... association, Bell's first communication by telephone was not 'Tom, come here, I want you', **(7)** .... 'Mr Watson, come here, I want you'.

(8) .... with excitement, Bell and Watson demonstrated their invention to a US telegram company. The company wrote to Bell, **(9)** .... that his invention was interesting. However, after **(10)** .... it careful consideration, they had **(11)** ... to the conclusion that it had 'no future'. Fortunately for Bell, others could see the possibilities. **(12)** .... four years of its invention, the US had 60,000 telephones. In the next twenty years that **(13)** .... increased to over 6 million.

⫸→

Today, ninety-three per cent of US homes have a phone, a **(14)** .... of phone ownership no other nation comes near to equalling. Each US household makes or receives **(15)** .... average 3,516 calls per year, an astonishing statistic.

1	**A**	in	**B**	with	**C**	to	**D**	out
2	**A**	joined	**B**	named	**C**	employed	**D**	applied
3	**A**	through	**B**	as	**C**	because	**D**	along
4	**A**	quite	**B**	just	**C**	simply	**D**	lately
5	**A**	managed	**B**	achieved	**C**	succeeded	**D**	fulfilled
6	**A**	narrow	**B**	attached	**C**	close	**D**	near
7	**A**	but	**B**	otherwise	**C**	instead	**D**	although
8	**A**	Whole	**B**	Deep	**C**	Entire	**D**	Filled
9	**A**	saying	**B**	informing	**C**	describing	**D**	referring
10	**A**	regarding	**B**	giving	**C**	taking	**D**	bearing
11	**A**	reached	**B**	come	**C**	arrived	**D**	brought
12	**A**	Under	**B**	From	**C**	Within	**D**	About
13	**A**	figure	**B**	count	**C**	measure	**D**	extent
14	**A**	grade	**B**	height	**C**	level	**D**	rank
15	**A**	on	**B**	by	**C**	at	**D**	for

Part 2

For Questions **16–30**, read the text below and think of the word which best fits each space. Use only **one** word in each space. There is an example at the beginning **(0)**. Write your answers **on the separate answer sheet**.

Example: | 0 | *there* |

WORKING IN ADVERTISING

If you want to work in advertising, **(0)** .... are three areas you can work in. The first is the Creative Department, which invents all the advertisements. Workers in **(16)** .... department are known as 'Creatives' and they always work **(17)** .... pairs. A creative job, **(18)** .... outsiders, might not sound very stressful, **(19)** .... the pressure to create original work is intense. Creatives have to keep up to **(20)** .... with the latest films, cartoons, videos, books and fashions to discover new techniques that could **(21)** .... used to sell a product.

The second area is the Accounts Department. This does **(22)** .... deal with financial accounts but with the companies that the agency produces advertisements for. Account Executives have to **(23)** .... sure that the Creatives fully understand **(24)** .... the client requires. Account Executives need to keep both the Creative team **(25)** .... the client happy. It's a job that requires a lot of diplomacy, as **(26)** .... as a very good memory and excellent organisational skills.

The third area is the media, which involves placing advertisements in magazines, **(27)** .... radio or TV, or in public areas. The Media Department carries **(28)** .... research into people's habits, to find out, for example, **(29)** .... radio stations long-distance lorry drivers prefer. Then it advises clients about which medium would be **(30)** .... appropriate for its advertisement.

Part 3

For Questions **31–40**, complete the second sentence so that it has a similar meaning to the first sentence, using the word given. **Do not change the word given**. You must use between two and five words, including the word given. There is an example at the beginning **(0)**.

Write **only** the missing words **on the separate answer sheet**.

Example:

0   My brother is too young to drive a car.

not

My brother .... drive a car.

The gap can be filled by the words 'is not old enough to' so you write:

0	*is not old enough to*

---

31   'Would you prefer to have a table by the window?' the waiter asked.

we

The waiter asked us .... to have a table by the window.

32   I'm getting bored here – let's go to a different place.

we

I'm getting bored here – why .... else?

33   I really didn't want to queue for tickets so I bought them by phone.

avoid

I was anxious .... for tickets, so I bought them by phone.

34   I couldn't decide whether I preferred the blue shirt or the green one.

choice

I couldn't .... the blue shirt and the green one.

35   Despite his disappointment, he continued to be cheerful.

remained

Although .... cheerful.

20

36 There were so many people on the train that I couldn't get a seat.
crowded

The train was .... nowhere for me to sit.

37 The price of the books was less than I had expected.
not

The books did .... I had expected.

38 My sister would never watch television until she had done her homework.
watching

My sister always .... television.

39 It appears that we have no bread left.
run

We seem to .... bread.

40 We last went to Spain three years ago.
years

It .... we last went to Spain.

Part 4

For Questions **41–55**, read the text below and look carefully at each line. Some of the lines are correct, and some have a word which should not be there.
If a line is correct, put a tick (✓) by the number **on the separate answer sheet**. If a line has a word which should **not** be there, write the word **on the separate answer sheet**. There are two examples at the beginning (**0** and **00**).

Examples:

0	*she*
00	**✓**

MY BEST FRIEND

0	I have several good friends but I suppose that my best friend she is
00	Ellen. We have been friends with each other since we were very young
41	because of she used to live next door to me. We have always been in the
42	same class at school, although she has always been much more cleverer
43	than me. I don't mind though, because she often helps me with my
44	homework! Anyway, I've always been better at sport than she is. I
45	always beat her at tennis and she doesn't like that. In fact, she hates
46	losing at anything and gets herself very annoyed if she does. That's the
47	only thing that i don't like it about her. Otherwise, she has a great sense of
48	humour and she's always making me to laugh. We get on very well
49	together, although occasionally we've had arguments – usually are about
50	silly little things. Ellen and with her family moved to another district
51	last year but I still see her a lot. We're planning to go on a trip around
52	Europe the next summer. I'm really looking forward to it because I think
53	sure we'll have a lot of fun and see exciting places. Of course, it's
54	going to be hard to afford us such a wonderful and exciting trip and
55	so we're both going to get jobs and try to save up enough money for it.

Part 5

For Questions **56–65**, read the text below. Use the word given in capitals at the end of each line to form a word that fits in the space in the same line.
There is an example at the beginning (**0**).
Write your answers **on the separate answer sheet**.

Example:

0	*existence*

BELLS

Bells have been in (**0**) .... for a long time. They were used by the   **EXIST**
(**56**) .... about 6,000 years ago and the oldest bell ever found is   **CHINA**
around 7,000 years old. Today, we live in a world of mass (**57**) ....   **COMMUNICATE**
and (**58**) .... clocks, so it is easy to forget what an essential part of   **RELY**
everyday life bells used to be.

Bells told people of happy events, such as weddings and (**59**) ....   **BORN**
or, sometimes had to announce (**60**) .... events such as a   **PLEASANT**
(**61**) .... or a funeral. Sometimes bells were used for giving people   **DIE**
(**62**) .... of an enemy's approach or spreading the good news of   **WARN**
victory.

In many places today, bells are perhaps most (**63**) .... associated   **COMMON**
with announcing when (**64**) .... services are going to take place.   **RELIGION**
They are also frequently rung during (**65**) .... and continue to play   **CELEBRATE**
a part in many people's lives.

PAPER 4   LISTENING (approximately 40 minutes)

Part 1

You will hear people talking in eight different situations. For Questions **1–8**, choose the best answer **A**, **B** or **C**.

---

1   You hear the weather forecast on the radio.
What is the weather going to be like today?

   A   getting brighter

   B   getting windier

   C   getting wetter

	1

2   You are listening to a trailer for a radio programme later this evening.
What is the programme about?

   A   music

   B   fashion

   C   films

	2

3   You hear a woman talking at a meeting about the environment.
What is she doing when she speaks?

   A   issuing a warning

   B   suggesting a solution

   C   making a protest

	3

4   You hear a woman talking about her job.
What is her present job?

   A   She trains people to use computers.

   B   She interviews people looking for jobs.

   C   She designs games to be played on computers.

	4

5 You hear part of a radio programme in which listeners can take part in a competition.
What is the prize?

A a book

B a film

C a map

> 5

6 Listen to this woman talking to her friend.
What does she think of the new restaurant?

A It has good service.

B It has good food.

C It is good value for money.

> 6

7 Listen to this man talking to his friend.
Why is he talking to her?

A to postpone a tennis game

B to arrange a dinner party

C to request some help

> 7

8 Listen to this woman talking about an interview.
How does she feel about it?

A confident

B annoyed

C disappointed

> 8

Part 2

You will hear a radio talk about a new educational and tourist attraction in the north of England. For Questions **9–18**, complete the notes which summarise what the speaker says.

Saxon Bridge Rainforest Centre

Near: _____ **9**

Set up in: _____ **10**

By: _____ **11**

Whole forest contained in: _____ **12**

Examples of plant species:

Passion flowers and _____ **13**

First house environment: lowland forest

Fifth house environment: _____ **14**

Centre wants to add: _____ **15** to its animal collection.

Special days for schools and scientists:

Mondays, _____ and _____ **16**

Admission charge for schools and disabled: _____ **17**

Saxon Bridge's symbol: _____ **18**

Part 3

You will hear five different people talking about a drama group which they are members of. For Questions **19–23**, choose which of the statements **A–F** best summarises what each speaker is saying. Use the letters only once. There is one extra letter which you do not need to use.

_____

A It's not like other groups.

Speaker 1	**19**

B I was persuaded to join.

Speaker 2	**20**

C This is the play we're doing now.

Speaker 3	**21**

D I needed a new hobby.

Speaker 4	**22**

E This is how the group was formed.

Speaker 5	**23**

F I learnt not to feel nervous.

Part 4

You will hear an interview with a man who has just returned from travelling. For Questions **24–30**, choose the best answer **A**, **B** or **C**.

24 The journey he made was

    A from the North to the South Pole.
    B across Africa.
    C across Europe and Asia.

	24

25 His main reason for making the journey was

    A to help him recover from an illness.
    B to raise money for charity.
    C to prove that he could do it.

	25

26 He stopped half way because

    A he met up with old friends.
    B he wanted to work.
    C he needed a rest.

	26

27 When he set off, his family felt

    A puzzled.
    B annoyed.
    C pleased.

	27

28 The worst incident on the journey was a meeting with

    A a customs officer.
    B a police officer.
    C a journalist.

	28

29 The media coverage of his journey was

    A worse than he expected.
    B better than he expected.
    C the same as he expected.

	29

30 What would he like to do next?

    A find an easier route
    B try a new walking route
    C travel over the same route again

	30

PAPER 5   SPEAKING (approximately 14 minutes)

You take the Speaking test with another candidate, referred to here as your partner. There are two examiners. One will speak to you and your partner and the other will just be listening. Both examiners will award marks.

Part 1 (3 minutes)

The examiner asks you and your partner questions about yourselves. You may be asked about things like 'your home town', 'your interests', 'your career plans', etc.

Part 2 (4 minutes)

The examiner gives you two photographs and asks you to talk about them for about one minute. The examiner then asks your partner a question about your photographs and your partner responds briefly.

Then the examiner gives your partner two different photographs. Your partner talks about these photographs for about one minute. This time the examiner asks you a question about your partner's photographs and you respond briefly.

Part 3 (3 minutes)

The examiner asks you and your partner to talk together. You may be asked to discuss something, solve a problem or perhaps come to a decision about something. For example, you might be asked to decide the best way to use some rooms in a language school. The examiner gives you a picture to help you but does not join in the conversation.

Part 4 (4 minutes)

The examiner joins in the conversation. You all talk together in a more general way about what has been said in Part 3. The examiner asks you questions but you and your partner are also expected to develop the conversation.

Test 2

PAPER 1   READING (1 hour 15 minutes)

Part 1

You are going to read a newspaper article about a company that manufactures diving equipment. Choose the most suitable summary sentence from the list **A–I** for each part (**1–7**) of the article. There is one extra summary sentence which you do not need to use. There is an example at the beginning (**0**).

Mark your answers **on the separate answer sheet**.

A	Satisfying safety controls was the most important concern.
B	Safety demands in the diving industry are growing rapidly.
C	Pressure came from other companies.
D	The company met the demands of a new market.
E	The success of the early years seemed likely to continue.
F	There are advantages for a small company.
G	A decision to change direction was made.
H	Preparations have been made to control the company size.
I	It started with a swim.

Well suited for shark-filled waters

0   *I*

FOR THE Brennan family, what began as a dip in the sea grew into a successful water sports business, which then went on to win a place for itself in the specialist water safety and survival market.

1

The family's interest in water sports began in 1965 and led to its decision to set up *Sea Sports* to supply the rapidly growing water leisure industry. Over the next seven years the business grew steadily, becoming a limited company in 1972. This was a time of expansion, particularly in Europe.

2

The firm then found itself under threat from cheaper imports. According to Jane Nye, daughter of the founder of the company, the competition forced them to lower their prices and highlighted the difficulties of a small manufacturing company whose products are easily copied. The company was forced to release half its 50-strong workforce. 'It was a serious blow as we had been growing. We were successful and then that came along,' Mrs Nye explained.

3

'It was agreed that we needed to move into the area of safety products for the diving industry,' she said. The company used its knowledge of the world of diving to find markets where there was little competition. 'The point about products in the safety and survival markets is that they are covered by regulations. Many companies do not have the quality systems that would satisfy these.'

4

In order to reach this specialist market, the company established a new department in 1979, to produce safety equipment. It won contracts to supply large organisations with emergency breathing equipment and tough sea wear. 'At that time, they were looking for better solutions to deep-sea diving and they came to companies like us and said "What can you do?" They liked the ideas that we put forward and so we got the work,' Mrs Nye said.

5

The long development process meant working closely with an institute of Health and Safety, and an institute of Naval Medicine as well as leading scientists in the field. 'You're talking about products that involve people so you have medical regulations and all kinds of procedures to go through in order to be able to develop products and do manned testing – all of that is a very lengthy and costly process,' Mrs Nye said.

6

Throughout, she has been determined to get the most from the workforce. The lines of communication within the company match its size. 'Everyone can talk to me; it's not as if the management is remote from the people who are working here – we are a unit that works together and the managers are all very accessible,' Mrs Nye said.

7

Now, with further growth in its sights, the group plans to take on extra staff but does not plan for a workforce of more than 75. 'We have concentrated on equipping people in the organisation with a lot of skills. We have trained and invested heavily in this so that staff can move wherever they are needed. We're a small specialist company – we'll grow but not out of proportion.'

Part 2

You are going to read an extract from a book about collecting animals for zoos. For Questions **8–14**, choose the answer (**A**, **B**, **C** or **D**) which you think fits best according to the text.

Mark your answers **on the separate answer sheet**.

ON ANY collecting trip, obtaining the animals is, as a rule, the simplest part of the job. As soon as the local people discover that you are willing to buy live wild creatures, the stuff comes pouring in; ninety per cent is, of course, the commoner types, but they do bring an occasional rarity. If you want the really rare stuff, you generally have to go out and find it yourself, but while you are devoting your time to this you can be sure that all the common local animals will be brought in to you. So one might also say that getting the animals is easy: the really hard part is keeping them once you have got them.

The chief difficulty you have when you have got a newly caught animal is not so much the shock it might be suffering, but the fact that being caught forces it to exist close to a creature it regards as an enemy of the worst possible sort: yourself. On many occasions an animal may take beautifully to being in a cage but getting used to the idea of living with people is another matter. This is the difficulty you can only deal with by patience and kindness. For month after month an animal may try to bite you every time you approach its cage, until you despair of ever making a favourable impression on it. Then, one day, sometimes without any preliminary warning, it will trot forward and take food from your hand, or allow you to tickle it behind the ears. At such moments you feel that all the waiting in the world was worthwhile.

Feeding, of course, is one of your main problems. Not only must you have a fairly extensive knowledge of what each animal eats in the wild state, but you have to work out something else when the natural food is unavailable, and then teach your animal to eat it.

You also have to provide for their individual likes and dislikes, which vary enormously. I have known a rat which, refusing all normal rat food – fruit, bread, vegetables – lived for three days on an exclusive diet of spaghetti. I have had a group of five monkeys, of the same age and types, who displayed the oddest individual characteristics. Out of the five, two loved hard-boiled eggs, while the other three were frightened of the strange white shapes and would not touch them, actually screaming in fear if you put such a terrifying object as a hard-boiled egg into their cage. These five monkeys all adored oranges but, whereas four would carefully peel their fruit and throw away the skin, the fifth would peel his orange equally carefully and then throw away the orange and eat the peel. When you have a collection of several hundred creatures all displaying such curious characteristics, you are sometimes driven mad in your efforts to satisfy their desires, and so keep them healthy and happy.

But of all the irritating tasks that you have to undertake during a collecting trip, bringing the baby animals up by hand is undoubtedly the worst. To begin with, they are generally stupid over taking a bottle and there is nothing quite so unattractive as struggling with a baby animal in a sea of warm milk. And then they have to be kept warm, especially at night, and this means (unless you take them to bed with you, which is often the answer) you have to get up several times during the night to refill hot-water bottles. After a hard day's work, to drag yourself out of bed at three in the morning to see to hot-water bottles is an occupation that soon loses its charm.

8   What does the writer say about getting hold of animals?
   A The best solution is to collect most of them yourself.
   B Dealing with local collectors takes a lot of time.
   C Collecting large numbers of animals is usually no problem.
   D Local people may not understand how rare some animals are.

9   What is the main problem with an animal that has just been caught?
   A It is frightened to be near humans.
   B It has been badly shocked by its experience.
   C It does not like being with other animals.
   D It will try to break out of its cage.

10   How does the writer treat new animals in his collection?
   A He keeps away from those that bite.
   B He tries to build up a relationship with them.
   C He feeds them by hand every day.
   D He keeps them separate for several months.

11   How does the writer make sure the animals have a good diet?
   A He collects food for them from their natural home.
   B He gives them a variety of fruit, bread and vegetables.
   C He mixes food they dislike in with their favourites.
   D He finds alternatives to their natural food if necessary.

12   What do we learn about the five monkeys?
   A Some of them did not want eggs in their cage.
   B One of them did not know how to peel an orange.
   C Some of them were too frightened to eat anything.
   D One of them threw his orange at the others.

13   The writer says that with a large collection of animals, it is
   A impossible to keep them all in cages.
   B a problem to control their natural curiosity.
   C crazy to expect them all to be healthy.
   D hard work to give each one what it wants.

14   What problem does the writer have at night?
   A He has to work with the baby animals until 3 a.m.
   B He keeps the baby animals' cages in his bedroom.
   C He has to keep getting up to look after the babies.
   D The babies have to be given regular warm drinks.

Part 3

You are going to read a newspaper article about a special course for people who are afraid of flying. Eight sentences have been removed from the article. Choose from the sentences **A–I** the one which fits each gap (**15–21**). There is one extra sentence which you do not need to use. There is an example at the beginning (**0**).
Mark your answers **on the separate answer sheet**.

All aboard the flight from fear

Stuart Rising was *terrified* of flying. And he was one of the relaxed ones on a course aimed at curing passengers of air-travel phobia.

About 200 of us assembled in the huge lecture room of the luxury Heathrow airport hotel. **0** *I* And we were about to take part in a fear-of-flying course: a seminar conducted by two airline pilots and a psychologist from a leading London hospital.

We sat like attentive schoolchildren, focused on our three teachers. First, we were asked to identify our specific fears and problems. Some did not like take-off and landing. **15** Some shared my intense dislike of being trapped in the seemingly small space of an aircraft.

Our first teacher asked: 'Does anyone dislike lifts or travelling on the Underground?' Lots of hands shot up with mine. I felt better already. One person had been struck by terror on an Underground train. **16** I was in good company.

Our tutor encouraged us to identify our particular worries and fears connected with air travel. We formed teams and got to know each other. **17** For example, the pilots explained that on take-off there is always a lot of noise as the engines build up power, but nothing is wrong.

The pilots discussed other common fears and worries. People like me, who may feel breathless in enclosed spaces, were reassured that the air in the aircraft is continually being changed. There is always enough air. **18** [ ] The principles of flight were discussed and the pilots explained that air travel is, in fact, one of the safest forms of modern transport.

The time had come. We were told to take all the positive action needed. We should be courageous and resolute. Now, if we followed through, we would be able to face our fear of flying and then overcome it.

We were taken to a 747 aircraft. We climbed aboard. I sat beside Betty, the lady who had panicked in the lift. Nervously gripping her armrests, Betty was now minus her smile. The young woman across the aisle from me was in tears. She was scared, but she was on the plane. The engines roared into life; the plane moved forward. **19** [ ] 'Fasten your seatbelts, please,' a silky female voice urged us. How could we resist? We did as we were told and kept our cool. Or tried to.

Suddenly, we had taken off. We were airborne. We flew from Heathrow airport to the south coast. Dungeness Power Station was clearly visible from the window. On the return to Heathrow, we took it in turn to visit the flight deck. **20** [ ]

After we had got off the plane, we burst into a display of emotion, triumphantly laughing and cheering while exchanging hugs and claps on the back. **21** [ ] We had all faced a serious problem and taken a giant step toward overcoming it. We felt sad for the few who had refused to board the aircraft. The chances are that they will probably never get on any plane.

Me? I'll soon be flying to America.

A Betty, a middle-aged lady with a lovely smile, admitted that she had panicked while stuck in a lift between floors in a Spanish hotel.

B Betty, delighted to be back on the ground, even gave me a friendly peck on the cheek.

C Everything there was under control and, of course, we understood that the 'bump' on landing was quite normal.

D No turning back now.

E More strange and potentially frightening noises occur at other times, such as when the wheels are pulled up.

F Others disliked the movement of the plane when it is hit by air currents.

G However, stress and tension can be brought on simply by shallow breathing: we were therefore encouraged always to take deep, full breaths.

H We were then ready to analyse our problems, which were discussed and critically examined.

I Young, middle-aged and old: what we all had in common was a fear of flying.

Part 4

You are going to read a review from a music magazine. For Questions **22–35**, choose from the albums reviewed (**A–E**). Some of the albums may be chosen more than once. When more than one answer is required, these may be given in any order. There is an example at the beginning (**0**).

Mark your answers **on the separate answer sheet**.

Of which album(s) are the following statements true?

Additional interesting material comes with the album.	**0**	*D*	
All the music is taken from public performances.	**22**		
Some of the music has not been heard in public before.	**23**		
The album contains music recorded after one of the performers died.	**24**		
One of the items has recently been a big hit.	**25**		
The new version of the album contains more items than the original.	**26**	**27**	
The album was produced after musical experiments.	**28**		
The recordings show how artists can find it difficult to keep up standards.	**29**	**30**	
The playing on the album lacks originality.	**31**		
The majority of the music does not live up to its description.	**32**		
The title of the album was taken from a programme about the performers.	**33**		
The original album was made to meet legal obligations.	**34**		
It is much better than similar albums.	**35**		

Re-releases

MIKE BURWOOD *looks at a selection of music albums which are making their second appearance on the recording scene.*

AMPLIFIED HEART
by Everything But The Girl   A

Most record buyers probably weren't even aware of this album's original release 18 months ago. Everything But The Girl's seventh studio LP created hardly any interest among a public for whom the band's brand of guitar-playing had long been little more than a feeble copy of other musicians. Re-released now, following the huge success of the popular single *Missing*, the album's selection of basically pointless songs seems more tired than ever. Only the new version of *Missing* makes any lasting impression and provides a reminder of the power once found at the heart of Everything But The Girl's music.

A GREAT DAY IN HARLEM
by Various Artists   B

At last, an alternative to the terrible collections so often sold as introductions to jazz! *A Great Day in Harlem* is based on a delightful documentary of the same name which tells the story of how some of the finest musicians in jazz history came to be photographed together in front of a New York building in 1958. Excellent examples of the work of 18 of them are found on 12 recordings with dates ranging from 1936 to 1994. Particular successes are Count Basie with his band, including Lester Young, and Charles Mingus's original version of *Goodbye Pork Pie Hat*, written in memory of the same Lester Young only two months after his death and less than a year after the original photo was taken.

⇒➔

HERE AND THERE
by Elton John

C

This was originally produced in 1976 simply to satisfy the requirements of Elton's contract with his record company. At that time, it consisted of ten songs put together from shows in London and New York, but it has now expanded to a 'greatest live hits' format with 16 more songs from those nights. Three of these – *Whatever Gets You Through The Night, Lucy in The Sky With Diamonds* and *I Saw Her Standing There* – feature John Lennon in his last onstage appearance.

WHO'S NEXT
by The Who

D

Considered by many to be the band's best, 1971's *Who's Next* was their only Number 1 album. Like many projects, it was developed from an earlier idea, in this case an attempt to combine rock-music opera with the limited technology of the time. With seven extra songs, four of them previously unreleased, notes by one of the band members and previously unseen photographs, this is definitely a collector's item.

KING OF THE DRUMS
by Sandy Nelson

E

Despite the enthusiasm of the accompanying notes, this album really centres on just one masterpiece – the 1961 instrumental hit *Let There Be Drums*, with its marvellous rhythms and rousing guitar-playing. *Let There Be Drums* actually followed another hit – the inferior *Teen Beat* – and Nelson spent the remainder of the 1960s trying unsuccessfully to produce similar hits. All these attempts are gathered among the 24 pieces here and this album provides a lesson in just how short a musician's stay at the top can be.

PAPER 2   WRITING (1 hour 30 minutes)

Part 1

You **must** answer this question.

1   You are studying English at Romsey College in Britain. A friend of yours in
    another country is going to the same college and has asked you for some
    information and advice.

    Read carefully the college information and the notes below. Then, using this
    information, write a letter to your friend telling her/him about next term. You
    may add other relevant points of your own.

ROMSEY COLLEGE – IMPORTANT DATES FOR NEXT TERM

Monday 6 Sept, Tuesday 7 Sept,
10.00–16.00: Course Registration

Tuesday 7 Sept, 9.00: College
bookshop opens

Wednesday 8 Sept, 9.15: First lesson

Wednesday 8 Sept: Welcome party from
20.00 at Seven Stars Hotel

Register as early as poss. Big queue, but worth it!

Need all books by Wed. Cost = £50 at bookshop.
NB have mine for 1/2 price!

First lesson – early (9.00) for good seat!

Party great fun

Write a **letter** of between **120** and **180** words in an appropriate style on the
next page. Do not write any addresses.

Part 1

Part 2

Write an answer to **one** of the questions **2–5** in this part. Write your answer in **120–180** words in an appropriate style on the next page. Put the question number in the box.

2   You have been asked to write an article for the college magazine which will help new students to organise their studies effectively. You need to include advice on study plans, good places to work in, exam preparation and making the best use of leisure time.

Write your **article**.

3   You see this advertisement in an international newspaper, which would give you the chance to spend the summer in Britain.

> ## Looking for a summer job?
>
> Friendly waiters and waitresses needed for our busy sea-front restaurant, popular with foreign visitors. No experience necessary but some knowledge of language an advantage. Fitness essential!
>
> Apply to: Mrs J Robinson, PO Box 100

Write your **letter of application.** Do not include addresses.

4   You have decided to enter a short-story competition organised by an international magazine. The competition rules say that the story must begin or end with the following words:

Bernie woke up suddenly and looked at the bed-side clock. It was three o'clock in the morning.

Write your **story**.

5   **Background reading texts**

Answer **one** of the following two questions based on your reading of **one** of the set books.

(a) Do you think the story you have read will be popular in 100 years' time? Write a **composition**, giving your opinion and reasons for your views.

(b) You have been invited to write a short article for your college magazine on the most interesting person in the book which you have read. Write your **article**, giving some details of that person's character and explaining why you find him or her especially interesting.

Part 2

Question	

....

....

....

....

....

....

....

....

....

....

....

....

....

....

....

....

....

....

....

....

....

....

....

....

....

....

....

PAPER 3   USE OF ENGLISH (1 hour 15 minutes)

Part 1

For Questions **1–15**, read the text below and decide which answer, **A**, **B**, **C** or **D** best fits each space. There is an example at the beginning (**0**).
Mark your answers **on the separate answer sheet**.

Example:

0   A sight   **B** look   **C** notice   **D** view

0	A	B	C	D
	▬	▭	▭	▭

AN UNUSUAL PLACE TO LIVE

Set in the red desert of central Australia is the mining town of Coober Pedy. At first **(0)** ...., the town looks **(1)** .... to many other such communities, but Coober Pedy is different. Sixty per cent of its population of some 4,000 people live underground. There are today about 800 underground houses as well as shops, hotels and even churches in the town and the **(2)** .... hills. Once a site has been chosen, special tunnelling machines are **(3)** .... in to create passages and rooms in the sandstone. Rock pillars are left to **(4)** .... the roof, and doors and windows are cut into the front. Houses are of all shapes and **(5)** ...., the largest having twenty rooms, and some even have their own swimming pool.

Living underground may **(6)** .... strange but in fact it has a **(7)** .... of advantages. In summer, the temperature outside can **(8)** .... an astonishing 47°C, and in winter the nights can be **(9)** .... cold. However, inside the houses it remains a steady 25°C all year **(10)** .... . Many people say that living underground **(11)** .... them feel very secure. There is no problem with noise from the neighbours and the houses are not **(12)** .... by the fierce dust storms that regularly **(13)** .... through the area. And of course, if your family **(14)** .... or lots of friends come to stay, you can **(15)** .... dig another room.

1	**A**	similar	**B**	like	**C**	same	**D**	alike
2	**A**	enclosing	**B**	close	**C**	near	**D**	surrounding
3	**A**	entered	**B**	brought	**C**	worked	**D**	placed
4	**A**	push	**B**	lift	**C**	rise	**D**	support
5	**A**	volumes	**B**	areas	**C**	sizes	**D**	numbers
6	**A**	consider	**B**	hear	**C**	suggest	**D**	sound
7	**A**	sum	**B**	plenty	**C**	number	**D**	total
8	**A**	achieve	**B**	reach	**C**	fulfil	**D**	hold
9	**A**	extremely	**B**	heavily	**C**	sharply	**D**	strongly
10	**A**	wide	**B**	round	**C**	across	**D**	along
11	**A**	makes	**B**	enables	**C**	allows	**D**	gets
12	**A**	spoiled	**B**	influenced	**C**	disturbed	**D**	affected
13	**A**	pour	**B**	sweep	**C**	flood	**D**	hurry
14	**A**	grows	**B**	rises	**C**	stretches	**D**	explodes
15	**A**	ever	**B**	regularly	**C**	always	**D**	only

Part 2

For Questions **16–30**, read the text below and think of the word which best fits each space. Use only **one** word in each space. There is an example at the beginning (**0**). Write your answers **on the separate answer sheet**.

Example:

0	*who*

THE DEVELOPMENT OF THE CAMERA

In 1877, George Eastman, **(0)** .... worked in a bank in Rochester, wanted to take photographs on holiday. However, he was very disappointed to discover that the only cameras available **(16)** .... very large and heavy, and required **(17)** .... use of complicated equipment.

Eastman realised that many other people were keen **(18)** .... take photographs but were prevented from **(19)** .... so. What was needed was a simple, hand-held camera, and so, in **(20)** .... spare time, he began to experiment.

After a **(21)** .... deal of work he was ready to open a factory and succeeded **(22)** .... producing his first camera in 1888. It was a small rectangular box and inside was a roll of special paper. This paper was sensitive to light and replaced the heavy pieces of glass that **(23)** .... been used before. When the roll was finished, the camera had to **(24)** .... sent back to the factory in New York **(25)** .... the photographs to be developed and printed. The following year a transparent film was invented **(26)** .... was better than the paper roll. This could be removed **(27)** .... the photographer and taken to a local centre for developing.

The new camera was **(28)** .... instant success and within a **(29)** .... years Eastman was very rich. But he was a generous man and during his lifetime he gave away millions of dollars to support a number **(30)** .... educational institutions.

Part 3

For Questions **31–40**, complete the second sentence so that it has a similar meaning to the first sentence, using the word given. **Do not change the word given**. You must use between two and five words, including the word given. There is an example at the beginning (**0**).

Write **only** the missing words **on the separate answer sheet**.

Example:

0 My brother is too young to drive a car.

not

My brother .... drive a car.

The gap can be filled by the words 'is not old enough to' so you write:

0	*is not old enough to*

---

31 The course finished with a big party.

end

At .... there was a big party.

32 Be careful or you'll hurt yourself.

if

You'll hurt yourself .... careful.

33 Finding suitable accommodation might be difficult.

find

It .... suitable accommodation.

34 The price of the holiday includes all meals.

included

All .... price of the holiday.

35 In my opinion, the problem has happened for two reasons.

are

In my opinion, ... this problem has happened.

36 'You broke my camera!' Susan said to Richard.
accused

Susan .... her camera.

37 You're going too fast for me.
keep

I .... you!

38 Where can I find the station?
how

Could you tell .... to the station?

39 Mary used to be better paid than she is these days.
as

These days Mary is .... she used to be.

40 I'm happy to go and see any film you choose.
mind

I .... we go and see.

Part 4

For Questions **41–55,** read the text below and look carefully at each line. Some of the lines are correct, and some have a word which should not be there.
If a line is correct, put a tick (✓) by the number **on the separate answer sheet**. If a line has a word which should be there, write the word **on the separate answer sheet.**
There are two examples at the beginning (**0** and **00**).

Examples:

0	✓

00	*being*

DIAMOND SPORTS CENTRE

0	Diamond is a modern sports centre which is ideal for people
00	of all ages. It is being situated on the outskirts of town near
41	Pennygold Park and is easy to get to it by bus. The centre has got an
42	indoor swimming pool and too there is a fully-equipped gymnasium.
43	There is a large sports hall with facilities for do a number
44	of team games such as the volleyball and basketball, as well
45	as have four outdoor tennis courts. The centre has six qualified
46	members of staff who are responsible for supervision and they
47	can offer advice on individual training programmes. They also
48	organise a full programme of variety competitions at different levels
49	of ability, which all members are encouraged to take part in.
50	There is a café with a good choice of so interesting and healthy
51	food, and you can enjoy a full meal, a snack or just to relax with
52	a refreshing drink. The centre is open up every day from 8.00 in
53	the morning until 10.00 in the evening. With specially reduced
54	membership type rates for students and retired people, the Diamond
55	Sports Centre offers excellent value for anybody who wanting to
	keep in good shape and make lots of new friends.

Part 5

For questions **56–65**, read the text below. Use the word given in capitals at the end of each line to form a word that fits in the space in the same line. There is an example at the beginning (**0**).

Write your word **on the separate answer sheet**.

Example:

0	*considerable*

PROBLEMS ON THE BUSES

People living in Croston have experienced a **(0)** .... number of   CONSIDER
difficulties this week **(56)** .... the local bus company's introduction   FOLLOW
of several new routes. There have been reports of **(57)** .... losing   DRIVE
their way and having to ask passengers for **(58)** .... when they have   DIRECT
had to go to parts of the town which were not **(59)** .... served by   PREVIOUS
buses. Not surprisingly, people have complained about the **(60)** ....   FAIL
of buses to arrive on time. Peter Gray, the **(61)** .... of the company   MANAGE
admits that the situation has been totally **(62)** .... this week and has   SATISFACTORY
(63) .... to passengers for the inconvenience caused. He believes   APOLOGY
that the company was probably being too **(64)** .... in introducing so   AMBITION
many new services on the same day. However, he is **(65)** .... that all   CONFIDENCE
the difficulties will have been sorted out by next week.

PAPER 4   LISTENING (approximately 40 minutes)

Part 1

You will hear people talking in eight different situations. For Questions **1–8**, choose the best answer **A**, **B** or **C**.

---

1   You overhear two friends talking about going to a party.
When is it?

   A   tonight

   B   tomorrow night

   C   next week

2   You overhear a customer talking to a saleswoman.
What does he want to buy?

   A   a shirt

   B   a suit

   C   a pair of trousers

3   Listen to this woman talking to her friend.
What is her intention?

   A   to request

   B   to persuade

   C   to suggest

4   Listen to this extract from a radio programme.
What sort of programme is it?

   A   a weather forecast

   B   a travel show

   C   a sports programme

5 You hear a man telling a story about a colleague who had an accident.
Where did the accident happen?

   A a sporting event

   B a music concert

   C a play at a theatre

	5

6 You hear a radio advertisement.
What is being advertised?

   A a disco

   B a social club

   C a means of transport

	6

7 You hear part of a programme about things to do in New York.
What type of place is being described?

   A a museum

   B a shop

   C a factory

	7

8 Listen to this man talking to a taxi driver.
Where is he going?

   A the airport

   B the theatre

   C the sports club

	8

Part 2

You will hear a telephone conversation where a woman asks for information about different study aids for the blind. For Questions **9–18**, complete the Enquiries Record.

BANSHIRE BLIND SOCIETY ENQUIRIES RECORD

Full name: _____ **9**

Course of study: _____ and _____ **10**

Braille proficiency: _____ **11**

Computer skills: _____ **12**

Type of equipment interested in: _____ **13**

and _____ **14**

Price range: from £____ to £____ **15**

Contact
Send message through (name): _____ **16**

Tel number: _____ **17**

Heard about us from: _____ **18**

Part 3

You will hear an advert for a travel insurance company where five people talk about bad experiences they have had whilst travelling. For Questions **19–23**, choose from the list **A–F** what each speaker is describing. Use the letters only once. There is one extra letter which you do not need to use.

A   some money was stolen

Speaker 1 | 19

B   a car broke down

Speaker 2 | 20

C   a car accident occurred

Speaker 3 | 21

D   a passport was stolen

Speaker 4 | 22

E   some luggage was stolen

Speaker 5 | 23

F   a car was stolen

Part 4

You will hear part of a radio programme about a problem caused by birds in a seaside town. For Questions **24–30**, decide whether the statements are **TRUE** or **FALSE**. Write **T** for **TRUE** or **F** for **FALSE**.

---

24 The sea birds like all kinds of food.

| | 24 |

25 The tourists find the birds entertaining.

| | 25 |

26 Local people used to want the birds in the town.

| | 26 |

27 The council's action may be making the problem worse.

| | 27 |

28 An expensive electronic system would solve the problem.

| | 28 |

29 A good solution is taking the eggs from the birds' nests.

| | 29 |

30 Egg-pricking would take a long time to work.

| | 30 |

PAPER 5   SPEAKING (approximately 14 minutes)

You take the Speaking test with another candidate, referred to here as your partner. There are two examiners. One will speak to you and your partner and the other will just be listening. Both examiners will award marks.

Part 1 (3 minutes)

The examiner asks you and your partner questions about yourselves. You may be asked about things like 'your home town', 'your interests', 'your career plans', etc.

Part 2 (4 minutes)

The examiner gives you two photographs and asks you to talk about them for about one minute. The examiner then asks your partner a question about your photographs and your partner responds briefly.

Then the examiner gives your partner two different photographs. Your partner talks about these photographs for about one minute. This time the examiner asks you a question about your partner's photographs and you respond briefly.

Part 3 (3 minutes)

The examiner asks you and your partner to talk together. You may be asked to discuss something, solve a problem or perhaps come to a decision about something. For example, you might be asked to decide the best way to use some rooms in a language school. The examiner gives you a picture to help you but does not join in the conversation.

Part 4 (4 minutes)

The examiner joins in the conversation. You all talk together in a more general way about what has been said in Part 3. The examiner asks you questions but you and your partner are also expected to develop the conversation.

Test 3

PAPER 1   READING (1 hour 15 minutes)

Part 1

You are going to read a magazine article about research into human weight. Choose from the list **A–H** the most suitable heading for each part of the article (**1–6**). There is one extra heading which you do not need to use. There is an example at the beginning (**0**).
Mark your answers **on the separate answer sheet**.

A	Isn't it boring?
B	The set menu for one, please
C	Initial impressions count
D	What happens to the volunteer
E	The way forward
F	Why take part?
G	What does it look like inside?
H	What *is* a calorimeter?

The Weight Experiment

Nicola Walters has been taking part in experiments in Scotland to discover why humans gain and lose weight. Being locked in a small room called a 'calorimeter' is one way to find out.

0	*H*

The signs above the two rooms read simply 'Chamber One' and 'Chamber Two'. These are the calorimeters: 4m by 2m white-walled rooms where human volunteers are imprisoned in the name of science. Outside these rooms another sign reads 'Please do not enter – work in progress' and in front of the rooms complicated machinery registers every move the volunteers make. Each day, meals measured to the last gram are passed through a hole in the wall of the calorimeter to the resident volunteer.

1

Despite the strange routine, there has never been a shortage of volunteers, male or female. Some even go back for a second stay. 'You can tell immediately if someone can cope' says researcher Alex Johnstone. 'You know the first time they open the door and stare inside. Some will instantly take a step back and say "I don't think I'd like that," and others will wander in and take a good look around.'

2

Nicola Walters is one of twenty volunteers who, over the past eight months, have spent varying periods inside the calorimeter. She was paid £40 for eight days of experiments, of which four were spent in the room. Tall and slim, Nicola does not have a weight problem, but thought the strict diet might help with her training and fitness programme. A self-employed community dance worker, she was able to fit the experiment in around her work. She saw an advert for volunteers at her local gym and as she is interested in the whole area of diet and exercise, she thought she would help out.

3

The experiment on Nicola involved her spending one day on a fixed diet at home and the next in the room. This sequence was repeated four times over six weeks. She arrived at the calorimeter at 8.30 am on each of the four mornings and from then on everything she ate or drank was carefully measured. Her every move was noted too, her

daily exercise routine timed to the last second. At regular intervals, after eating, she filled in forms about how hungry she felt and samples were taken for analysis.

4

The food, she insists, was tasty but the meals looked odd because they had been weighed and measured to the last ingredient. It takes three or four people to prepare each one, such is the level of accuracy needed. And when the time comes to eat, the volunteers are faced with plates of food chopped into all sorts of odd sizes.

5

The scientists help the volunteers impose a kind of order on the long days they face in the room. 'The first time, I only took one video and a book, but it was OK because I watched television the rest of the time,' says Nicola. And twice a day she used the exercise bike. She pedalled for half an hour, watched by researchers to make sure she didn't go too fast.

6

It seems that some foods encourage you to eat more, while others satisfy you quickly. Volunteers are already showing that high-fat diets are less likely to make you feel full. Believing that they may now know what encourages people to overeat, the researchers are about to start testing a high-protein weight-loss diet. Volunteers are required and Nicola has signed up for further sessions.

Part 2

You are going to read an article about a course for radio presenters. For Questions **7–14**, choose the answer (**A**, **B**, **C** or **D**) which you think fits best according to the text.
Mark your answers **on the separate answer sheet**.

There are 25 of us on the course for radio programme presenters, to hear the tips from the expert, Paul Fairburn, programme director at the station Heart FM. I have been doing the job for nearly 20 years but it is the closest I have ever come to anything like training. Two of us old hands are clearly there for the chance to make fun of radio presenter school (Lesson Five: The Time Check. 'Class, repeat after me: It's 21 minutes before the hour of three o'clock.').

About half of us are presenters from small local stations and the rest are the type of young man – they are always male – who is always, and a little unfairly, laughed at in the radio business: single-minded enthusiasts who in any other branch of entertainment would probably be welcomed.

Fairburn passes on a vital hint for potential phone-in hosts: 'Don't worry if someone phones up and says they're going to thump you. They won't. The people who are really going to hit you don't tell you first.' This is not altogether encouraging, but interesting to know, and we dutifully make a note of it. We also note Fairburn's tip number one: 'Get a Life outside radio.' 'If you are an interesting person, you will be a more interesting presenter,' says Fairburn. 'So don't spend all your time in radio stations.' This is a bit ironic, because if we had a life we probably wouldn't be sitting in that room on a Wednesday afternoon taking notes. For those of us who went into radio back in the 1970s, it may be a little late for all this. But times have changed, says Fairburn and now you need to learn the profession.

To this end, today's presenters will almost certainly be invited to spend time at lectures, learning from the masters. Dan O'Day, an American breakfast-show presenter generally regarded as one of the best of that kind, hosts weekend schools, at which topics such as 'Establishing Good Relations On The Telephone' are discussed deeply. The Metro Radio Group in Britain even makes its presenters sign an agreement not to give away confidential ideas picked up on the group's training schemes.

However, courtesy of Fairburn, who picked it up from a former Metro trainee, I am now able to reveal exclusively one of those secrets. 'You are ten minutes from the end of a four-hour programme,' Fairburn tells the class. 'You are naturally winding down, sounding tired; so, a second or two before opening the microphone, shout "Wow!" very loudly into the closed microphone. Then, when you open it, you will sound wide awake, despite yourself.' It does work. I have tried it since, although "Wow!" doesn't seem like the right word for the station I work on, so I tend to shout "Heck!"

Another example of presenter cleverness, which never occurred to us older ones, is the phone-in trick. This gets you on good terms with the local audience if you find yourself working in a strange town. When someone phones in, you find out in some detail – before putting them on the air – where they come from, what the local landmarks are and so on. Then, when they appear on the radio and say where they are calling from, you can say authoritatively, 'Oh yes, just around the corner from the railway station.'

Brilliant, and much more practical than any advice I was given in the dark days when I started. With the benefit of an afternoon's training, I can see the old-fashioned attitudes that were passed on to me then have no place in today's highly competitive radio market.

3E

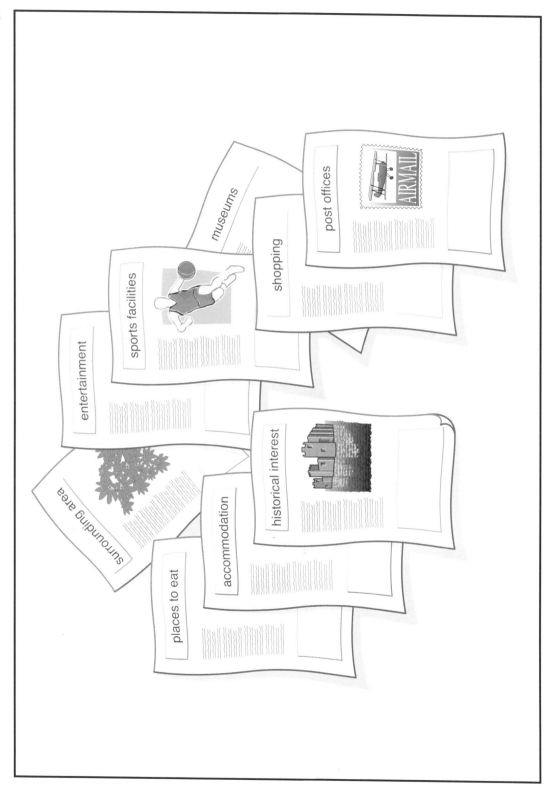

4E

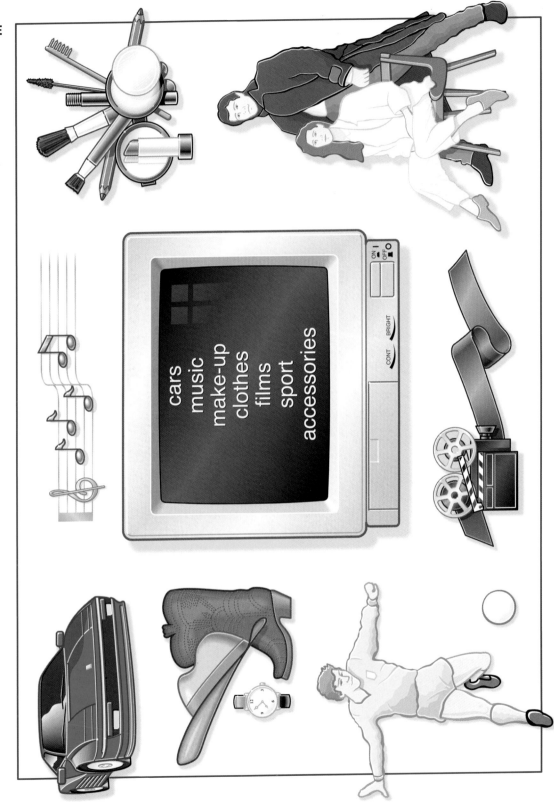

cars
music
make-up
clothes
films
sport
accessories

7 What do we learn about the writer in the first paragraph?
  A He had heard that this particular course wasn't very good.
  B He was attending the course so that he could write about it.
  C He wasn't given training as a radio presenter when he started.
  D He had always avoided courses for radio presenters before.

8 What does the writer say about some of the others taking the course?
  A People who work in radio have a low opinion of them.
  B They are never likely to find work as presenters.
  C They couldn't follow even simple instructions.
  D People who know them enjoy their programmes.

9 What does the writer say about the advice to phone-in hosts?
  A It was worth writing down.
  B It was not true of his own experience.
  C It was not intended for older presenters.
  D It was difficult to understand.

10 What do we learn about Metro Radio?
  A Paul Fairburn used to work there.
  B It runs courses for radio presenters.
  C It has copied American methods.
  D Excellent presenters work for it.

11 Where do 'those secrets' (line 51) originally come from?
  A confidential documents
  B radio programmes
  C telephone conversations
  D training schemes

12 What does the writer say about shouting into a closed microphone?
  A He has adapted the original idea.
  B He initially thought it wouldn't work.
  C It doesn't help him overcome problems.
  D He had tried a similar thing before.

13 What does the writer think of the 'phone-in trick'?
  A It works better in some places than in others.
  B It is wrong to deceive the listeners in that way.
  C It is a very good idea he hadn't thought of.
  D It requires too much research before the show.

14 What is the writer's conclusion after taking the course?
  A Such courses can be useful even for presenters with his experience.
  B He is glad that he started presenting radio programmes a long time ago.
  C Courses for radio presenters are unlikely to make them better at the job.
  D It has made him worried about his future career as a radio presenter.

Part 3

You are going to read a newspaper article by a British student who worked at a summer camp in the US. Seven paragraphs have been removed from the article. Choose from the paragraphs **A–H** the one which fits each gap (**15–20**). There is one extra paragraph which you do not need to use. There is an example at the beginning (**0**).
Mark your answers **on the separate answer sheet**.

Summer camp: a soap opera

Every June, thousands of British students fly to the United States to spend their holidays working at summer camps. In return, they get a free return flight, full board, pocket money and the chance to travel. Lucy Graham joined a camp and spent eight weeks working with six to sixteen-year-olds.

I APPLIED at the last minute and was so thrilled at the prospect of spending the holidays doing something more exciting than working in the local supermarket that I hastily accepted the only job left – in the camp laundry.

0	*H*

On arrival I was told by the camp director that I would be doing the washing for 200 children – on my own. Any romantic dreams I'd had quickly turned into nightmare reality. For the first week, the party sent out by the jobs agency – nine students, including me – became a full-time cleaning squad, getting the place ready for its grand opening.

15	

The children's arrival also brought 50 American counsellors to look after them, and the opening of the laundry. At first, I had to work from 8.45 in the morning till 10.30 at night to get all my work done. Considering there was no hot water in the laundry and the machines were old, the washing came out remarkably well.

16	

The kitchen workers, maintenance man and myself found that we were on the lowest level of the camp's class system. Our four British counsellor friends had a much better time. They got friendly with their American colleagues and were respected by the children. They were also given tips by parents after the holiday.

17

As for the camp itself, it had a large lake and excellent sporting facilities. But because organised activities for the children carried on into the evening, we usually didn't get the chance to use them. However, much more annoying were my room-mates, three 18-year-old girls who worked in the dining room.

18

On top of that, the camp food was poor, with child-size portions; fresh fruit and vegetables were rare. One catering worker even stood over the pineapple rings, checking that you took only one each.

19

However, I couldn't set off as soon as the children left because we had to stay on for a few days, cleaning and closing down the camp. My last duty was to load up the rubbish bags and take out any clothes the children had thrown away, in case their parents asked about them.

20

What's more, without the free ticket I got to the US – and the rail ticket from my parents – I would never have seen Niagara Falls, gone up the Empire State Building or had my picture taken with Mickey Mouse at Disney World.

A They had never been away from home before, and spent most of the night screaming with excitement. Sometimes, the only way to get any rest was to pretend to be ill and sleep in the medical centre.

B We weren't so lucky. We were never invited to join in the evening activities. When we did manage to get out of the camp, our evenings tended to consist of eating ice-cream at the local gas station.

C As a result, the standard of the camp you end up in is usually a question of luck. However, the agencies do hold meetings where you can ask representatives from camps about the facilities and the nature of the work you will be expected to do.

D We swept out the bedrooms and scrubbed the lavatories, gymnasium and kitchen. We polished the cooking equipment, put up the sports nets and carried any luggage sent on ahead to the bedrooms.

E On the whole it had been well worth it. Despite the washing, the camp's plus points had been a beautiful setting, meeting a great bunch of travelling companions and doing far more reading for my university course than I would have done at home.

F All these disadvantages meant that Saturdays, our days off, were highly valued. The places we visited then, such as New York City, gave me an appetite for travelling later on. If I hadn't done that, I would have regretted it – there is so much to see and do and I was keen to get on with it.

G But with so many clothes to wash and dry, some did get mixed up. I had six-year-olds marching up and telling me that their parents would be very angry if I didn't find their favourite sweater.

H I started to have my doubts while squashed between the swimming instructor and the sports teacher during the three-hour minibus ride to the camp, which was in a tiny town about 90 miles from New York City.

Part 4

You are going to read an article about sporting activities. For Questions **21–35**, choose
from the activities (**A–E**). Some of the activities may be chosen more than once. There is
an example at the beginning (**0**).
Mark your answers **on the separate answer sheet**.

Of which activity are the following stated?

You can do it whenever you want to.	**0**	*B*

You may not have to pay to do it.	**21**

You can develop a strong interest in it after doing it for the first time.	**22**

Everyone who does it has a similar attitude to life.	**23**

It may be physically unpleasant sometimes.	**24**

It shows you that you can do things you didn't think you were capable of.	**25**

It doesn't appeal to some people.	**26**

It requires you to work things out in advance.	**27**

It allows you to see places you otherwise wouldn't be able to see.	**28**

Everyone who takes part in it is considered equal.	**29**

Anyone who does it can make a mistake.	**30**

You don't have to take anything with you to do it.

31	

Learning it is similar to another experience you may have had.

32	

There are various tasks which are carried out for you during it.

33	

Being relied upon by others is part of it.

34	

There is an activity related to it which doesn't take long to learn.

35	

GET ACTIVE

SAILING A

As a sailing instructor, it is my experience that, while people who go sailing may have different professional lives and widely differing backgrounds, they all have one thing in common – they are all fun-loving, sociable and determined to get the most out of what they do.

The great thing about sailing is that you have to live and work together and it is a great leveller, wiping out differences in age, background and sex. There is no favouritism and no discrimination.

Sailing a yacht can be demanding, tiring, frustrating and wet. But it is also challenging, exciting, relaxing and wonderfully fulfilling. No experience is necessary and wet-weather and safety equipment is provided by schools, so all you need to bring is yourself. I can guarantee you will have a memorable time.

WALKING B

A walking holiday is not the most luxurious of trips but it does offer an opportunity to see remote areas of the world which cannot be visited any other way. And at the end of the day it gives you a wonderful sense of achievement. Camping is often part of this type of holiday and the joy is exploring totally uncivilised territory.

Don't worry, you don't have to carry your own luggage, only a day pack, as cook and camp teams do the everyday work, leaving you free to enjoy the experience. There's a destination for every time of the year, so when you go is up to you. So get those boots out and walk the world. ⋙→

ROCK CLIMBING   C

You don't have to be super-fit to go rock climbing; technique is more important than strength. It is also vital to plan and think ahead, as the easiest move may not always be the best. What often looks like an impossible situation, with a little thought and a few small steps, becomes achievable and before you know it you are half way up a mountain.

You cannot climb without a safety system as even the best people can slip. Even beginners are expected to operate the safety system. It's a frightening thought being responsible for another person's safety, and just as challenging is knowing that you are totally dependent on the safety system. This is the perfect team-building exercise.

FLYING   D

Within an hour you can be handling the controls of a light aircraft. After your instructor has given you details on the aircraft, its controls and where you are going to fly, you take off and climb to around 2000ft. You will then be allowed the chance to fly the plane itself. Not to worry. As when you learn to drive, the instructor has a set of controls too. An hour's lesson costs £95 and counts towards a private pilot's licence if, like many people, you find that you want to take up flying seriously. So if you fancy being a bird, this could be the nearest thing to it.

PARACHUTE JUMPING   E

Jumping from an aircraft may not be everyone's idea of fun, but if this is what you fancy, there is no excitement like it. And if you can raise money for charity by doing it, your jump could be free. You don't need a great deal of physical fitness but the training leading up to it requires that you be normally fit. Training involves practising the correct body position for landing, and emergency drills. Another fun activity in the sky is sky-diving, which involves jumping from an aircraft and falling a long way before opening the parachute. Tandem skydiving – jumping from the plane attached to an experienced instructor – requires only basic training, whereas attempting a solo jump requires months of practice.

PAPER 2 WRITING (1 hour 30 minutes)

Part 1

You **must** answer this question.

1   You and three friends have decided to go on a boating holiday in Wales. You have found an advertisement for Brecon Boating Holidays and you decide to find out more about these holidays.

Read carefully the advertisement below, on which you have made some notes. Then, using this information, write a letter to the company covering all your points. You may add other relevant information of your own.

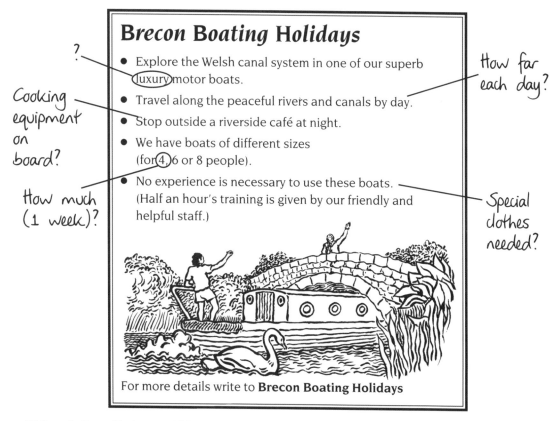

Brecon Boating Holidays

?

- Explore the Welsh canal system in one of our superb (luxury) motor boats.

Cooking equipment on board?

- Travel along the peaceful rivers and canals by day.
- Stop outside a riverside café at night.

How much (1 week)?

- We have boats of different sizes (for 4, 6 or 8 people).
- No experience is necessary to use these boats. (Half an hour's training is given by our friendly and helpful staff.)

How far each day?

Special clothes needed?

For more details write to **Brecon Boating Holidays**

Write **a letter** of between **120** and **180** words in an appropriate style on the next page. Do not write any addresses.

Part 1

Part 2

Write an answer to **one** of the questions **2–5** in this part. Write your answer in **120–180** words in an appropriate style on the next page. Put the question number in the box.

2 You have decided to enter a short story competition organised by an international young people's magazine. The competition rules say that the story must begin or end with the following words:

Without saying a word, Jo stood up and walked out of the room.

Write your **story**.

3 Colleges in your area recently took part in an important sporting event (for example, a tennis or football tournament, or an athletics competition). The results of your own college were much better than expected and you have decided to write an article about the events for your college magazine.

Write your **article**.

4 You work occasionally for an international travel company as a tour guide in your town. Recently you took a group of elderly visitors from another country on a tour round some of the most important buildings in your town. Now you must write a report on the tour for your boss. Include your suggestions for similar tours in the future.

Write your **report**.

5 **Background reading texts**

Answer **one** of the following two questions based on your reading of **one** of the set books.

(a) Choose an actor or actress who you think could play the part of your favourite character in the book you have read. Write a **composition**, stating who the character is and giving reasons for your choice of actor or actress.

(b) You have read about several events and situations in the book which you have chosen. Do you think that any of those events or situations could happen in your own country nowadays? Write a **composition**, explaining why or why not.

Part 2

Question	

....
....
....
....
....
....
....
....
....
....
....
....
....
....
....
....
....
....
....
....
....
....
....
....
....
....

PAPER 3   USE OF ENGLISH (1 hour 15 minutes)

Part 1

For Questions **1–15**, read the text below and decide which answer, **A**, **B**, **C** or **D** best fits each space. There is an example at the beginning (**0**).
Mark your answers **on the separate answer sheet**.

Example:

0 A for   **B** on   **C** to   **D** at

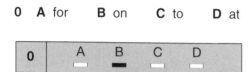

SEASIDE HOLIDAYS IN BRITAIN

British families started going **(0)** .... holiday to the seaside around the middle of the 19th century. The invention of the railways **(1)** .... this possible. The first holidaymakers were quite rich and went for their health and education. The seaside was a place to be **(2)** .... of illness, and doctors recommended bathing in the sea and drinking sea water. Also to **(3)** .... their knowledge, families attended concerts and read books from the library.

At that time, ordinary working people had very little time **(4)** .... work. However, in 1871, the government **(5)** .... four 'Bank Holidays' – national holiday days. This **(6)** .... people to have a day or two out, which **(7)** .... gave them a **(8)** .... for leisure and the seaside. At first, they went on day-trips, taking **(9)** .... of special cheap tickets on the railways.

By the 1880s, rising incomes **(10)** .... that many ordinary workers and their families could have a week's holiday at the seaside. Rail fares were reduced and cheap hotels were built to **(11)** .... them. Holidaymakers enjoyed being **(12)** .... , sitting on the beach, bathing in the sea, and eating ice-cream. Cheap entertainment was **(13)** .... offer and holidaymakers went to **(14)** .... fun.

Today, the English seaside **(15)** .... popular, with more than 18 million holidays taken there each year.

1	A	let	B	made	C	got	D	had
2	A	cured	B	remedied	C	recovered	D	improved
3	A	raise	B	spread	C	increase	D	add
4	A	out	B	off	C	away	D	from
5	A	installed	B	presented	C	introduced	D	brought
6	A	allowed	B	provided	C	offered	D	opened
7	A	hardly ever	B	here and there	C	seldom	D	now and then
8	A	taste	B	sense	C	favour	D	pleasure
9	A	benefit	B	opportunity	C	advantage	D	profit
10	A	caused	B	produced	C	meant	D	resulted
11	A	accommodate	B	board	C	cater	D	lodge
12	A	idle	B	easy	C	restful	D	spare
13	A	in	B	for	C	to	D	on
14	A	get	B	have	C	take	D	make
15	A	remains	B	stays	C	continues	D	lasts

Part 2

For Questions **16–30**, read the text below and think of the word which best fits each space. Use only **one** word in each space. There is an example at the beginning (**0**). Write your answers **on the separate answer sheet**.

Example:

0	*a*

THE BAREFOOT MAILMEN

In 1885, the US Post Office had **(0)** .... problem in the southern state of Florida. The delivery service **(16)** .... Lake Worth to Biscayen Bay was taking six weeks.

They found a solution – a 136-mile route **(17)** .... took three days. It meant that the mailmen **(18)** .... to walk barefoot along beaches for eighty miles and then cover **(19)** .... remaining fifty-six miles by boat. This difficult job was first carried **(20)** .... by mailman Edwin R Bradley. In the summer of 1887, James 'Ed' Hamilton **(21)** .... over deliveries but a few months later his career ended suddenly in circumstances which **(22)** .... him famous in the Post Office.

The Autumn weather **(23)** .... year was severe. On 9th October, Hamilton felt unwell as he set **(24)** ..... Despite this, he arrived at his first stop, Orange Grove. His next call should **(25)** .... been at a place called Fort Lauderdale Refuge. This time he didn't arrive **(26)** .... he was never seen again. Nobody ever found out **(27)** .... happened to him.

In 1892, a road was built and the days of the barefoot mailmen **(28)** .... over. However, their story has never been forgotten. **(29)** .... are annual walks along the route, and a book and film have **(30)** .... made about them.

Part 3

For Questions **31–40**, complete the second sentence so that it has a similar meaning to the first sentence, using the word given. **Do not change the word given.** You must use between two and five words, including the word given. There is an example at the beginning (**0**).
Write **only** the missing words **on the separate answer sheet**.

Example:

0 My brother is too young to drive a car.
   not

   My brother .... drive a car.

The gap can be filled by the words 'is not old enough to' so you write:

0	*is not old enough to*

---

31 We took a train to Liverpool last Saturday.
   by

   We .... last Saturday.

32 She did not thank us for our help when she left.
   us

   She left .... help.

33 We are hoping that the weather will improve next week.
   better

   We are hoping .... weather next week.

34 Who has to lock the doors when the office closes?
   responsible

   Who .... the doors when the office closes?

35 I was really pleased that at last my father had managed to give up smoking.
   successful

   I was really pleased that at last my father .... up smoking.

36 I went to sleep immediately the train left the station.
asleep

I .... as the train left the station.

37 It's unlikely that I'll see you again this week.
probably

We .... other again this week.

38 It will be nice to see you again at the party.
looking

I'm .... again at the party.

39 I haven't forgotten any of the details of what happened that day.
still

I .... detail of what happened that day.

40 We lost our way because the signposts were confusing.
caused

The signposts were confusing, which .... lost.

Part 4

For Questions **41–55**, read the text below and look carefully at each line. Some of the lines are correct, and some have a word which should not be there.
If a line is correct, put a tick (✓) by the number **on the separate answer sheet**. If a line has a word which should not be there, write the word **on the separate answer sheet**. There are two examples at the beginning (**0** and **00**).

Examples:

0	✓
00	*of*

THE BEATLES

0	In the 1960s, The Beatles were probably the most famous pop group in the
00	whole world. Since then, there have been a great many of groups that have
41	achieved enormous fame, so it is perhaps difficult now to imagine that how
42	sensational The Beatles were at the time. They were four boys from the
43	north of England and none of them had any kind training in music. They
44	started by performing and recording songs by black Americans and they had
45	done some success with these songs. Then they started writing their own
46	songs and that it was when they became really popular. The Beatles
47	changed pop music. They were the first one pop group to achieve great
48	success from songs they had written them themselves. After that it became
49	common for groups and singers to write their own songs. The Beatles did not
50	have a so long career. Their first hit record was in 1963 and they split up in
51	1970. They stopped doing live performances in 1966 because it had
52	become too much dangerous for them – their fans were so excited that they
53	surrounded them and tried to take their clothes as the souvenirs! However,
54	today some of their songs remain as famous as they were when they
55	first came out. Throughout in the world, many people can sing part of a
	Beatles song if you ask them.

Part 5

For Questions **56–65**, read the text below. Use the word given in capitals at the end of
each line to form a word that fits in the space in the same line.
There is an example at the beginning (**0**).
Write your answers **on the separate answer sheet**.

Example:

0	*popularity*

JUDO

Judo is a sport that has achieved great (**0**) .... in many parts of the	**POPULAR**
world. It was (**56**) .... developed in Japan in the late 19th century	**ORIGIN**
based on ancient methods of self-defence. There are two (**57**)	**FIGHT**
Although they use physical (**58**) .... against each other, they are	**VIOLENT**
(**59**) .... to their opponent and bow to each other before and after	**RESPECT**
each contest.	

Judo is an (**60**) .... sport to take up because the only equipment you	**EXPENSIVE**
need is the special loose-fitting suit. It is very suitable for (**61**) .... if	**YOUNG**
they join a club where the (**62**) .... are properly qualified and pay	**INSTRUCT**
enough attention to safety. Although Judo is a physically (**63**)	**DEMAND**
sport which requires a lot of (**64**) ...., practice and skill, there are	**STRONG**
many people who find it (**65**) .... as a means of relaxation in their	**ENJOY**
spare time.	

PAPER 4   **LISTENING** (approximately 40 minutes)

Part 1

You will hear people talking in eight different situations. For Questions **1–8**, choose the best answer **A**, **B** or **C**.

1   Listen to this girl talking about her new boss.
     How did she feel after she met him?

    A   delighted

    B   disappointed

    C   relieved

	1

2   You overhear two friends talking about a birthday present one of them has just received.
     What is it?

    A   a television

    B   a cassette player

    C   a computer

	2

3   You overhear two friends talking about a garden party they attended.
     What was the problem?

    A   the people

    B   the weather

    C   the place

	3

4   On a visit to a college, you overhear part of a lesson.
     What is the subject of the lesson?

    A   health and safety

    B   child development

    C   food preparation

	4

5 Listen to this critic talking about a film.
What sort of film is it?

   A   a comedy

   B   a romance

   C   a thriller

	5

6 Listen to this boy talking to a friend about flying.
How does he feel about flying?

   A   excited

   B   depressed

   C   scared

	6

7 You hear an artist talking about her work.
What type of artist is she?

   A   a photographer

   B   a sculptor

   C   a painter

	7

8 Listen to this woman leaving a phone message.
Why is she phoning?

   A   She is complaining about something.

   B   She is requesting something.

   C   She is apologising about something.

	8

Part 2

You will hear Ian Anderson of the Shoppers' Association talking about a problem people may face when buying some kinds of goods. For Questions **9–18**, complete the notes.

Problem:

Goods may be: [_____ 9]

Cause: Shops give customers [_____ 10]

Why people return goods: they are faulty

[_____ 11]

Main type of goods involved: [_____ 12]

Example: [_____ 13] sold as 'Manager's Special'

Repairer found: [_____ 14] inside.

Advice:

Be careful of:

expressions like 'Manager's Special' or [_____ 15]

[_____ 16] missing.

[_____ 17] damaged.

Main advice: Always [_____ 18]

Part 3

You will hear five people talking about what they did on holiday. For Questions **19–23**, choose from the list of activities **A–F** which each of them is describing. Use the letters only once. There is one extra letter which you do not need to use.

A skiing

                         Speaker 1 | | **19** |

B horse riding

                         Speaker 2 | | **20** |

C sightseeing

                         Speaker 3 | | **21** |

D walking

                         Speaker 4 | | **22** |

E cycling

                         Speaker 5 | | **23** |

F sailing

Part 4

You will hear part of a radio programme about people who become rich quickly. Ann is telling her story. For Questions **24–30** decide whether the statements are **TRUE** or **FALSE**. Write **T** for **TRUE** or **F** for **FALSE**.

---

24   Ann thinks her parents are educated people.

| | 24 |

25   Ann enjoyed writing novels.

| | 25 |

26   Ann's friends joked with her about the money.

| | 26 |

27   Ann gave her family some of the money.

| | 27 |

28   Ann was surprised at her family's reaction to the money.

| | 28 |

29   Ann says she learned most about writing from fellow students.

| | 29 |

30   Ann owns a successful publishing company.

| | 30 |

PAPER 5   SPEAKING (approximately 14 minutes)

You take the Speaking test with another candidate, referred to here as your partner. There are two examiners. One will speak to you and your partner and the other will just be listening. Both examiners will award marks.

Part 1 (3 minutes)

The examiner asks you and your partner questions about yourselves. You may be asked about things like 'your home town', 'your interests', 'your career plans', etc.

Part 2 (4 minutes)

The examiner gives you two photographs and asks you to talk about them for about one minute. The examiner then asks your partner a question about your photographs and your partner responds briefly.

Then the examiner gives your partner two different photographs. Your partner talks about these photographs for about one minute. This time the examiner asks you a question about your partner's photographs and you respond briefly.

Part 3 (3 minutes)

The examiner asks you and your partner to talk together. You may be asked to discuss something, solve a problem or perhaps come to a decision about something. For example, you might be asked to decide the best way to use some rooms in a language school. The examiner gives you a picture to help you but does not join in the conversation.

Part 4 (4 minutes)

The examiner joins in the conversation. You all talk together in a more general way about what has been said in Part 3. The examiner asks you questions but you and your partner are also expected to develop the conversation.

Test 4

PAPER 1 READING (1 hour 15 minutes)

Part 1

You are going to read a newspaper article about working as a conductor on a British train. Choose the most suitable heading from the list **A–I** for each part (**1–7**) of the article. There is one extra heading which you do not need to use. There is an example at the beginning (**0**). Mark your answers **on the separate answer sheet**.

A	Job satisfaction
B	Getting started in the job
C	Calling for help
D	Looking after the passengers
E	Keeping in touch
F	Ready for duty
G	Dealing with danger
H	There and back again
I	Time to get up

Train conductor

Ticket checks, travel questions and making sure passengers reach their destination safely are all part of a day's work for senior conductor Julie King.

0	*I*

The earliest shift we do starts at 4.30 in the morning, so if I'm on that one, I'll get up at three and watch a bit of TV to catch up on the news before driving to work. If I'm starting at nine, I can have a lie-in.

1	

I'm based on the Portsmouth to London line and the first thing I do is report to the supervisor, who makes sure we're fit for work. Then I pick up my ticket machine, read all the notices to check nothing's happened overnight I'm not aware of, have a cup of tea, collect my work schedule and make sure my train book is in order – we have to write down each stop on every trip. After that it's down to the platform to put my kit in the conductor's van and start the day.

2	

A typical day would be two return trips between Portsmouth and London. We aim to walk through the train after every stop, checking tickets and counting heads. Sometimes we walk through just to make sure everything's all right. Once we reach London, we take a 20-minute break to clear our heads before setting off on the return journey. When we get back to Portsmouth, I'll make sure the train is cleaned, then it's up to London again with more ticket checks and more announcements to passengers.

3	

A lot of the job is about customer care. We deal with all sorts of questions and can find out the information passengers want somehow. We carry timetables and fare books, and if we're asked something we can't find out on the spot, we use the phone on the train to ring the information office. We can also organise taxis for people if trains have been cancelled or are late and there is no alternative train service for them to get home on.

4	

The electronic communicators we carry are used to let us know about any problems with the service – not just on that line but on other routes as well. If it's important, we'll pass the information on to the passengers in a public announcement. The communicator doesn't make a sound and only I'm aware of it going off. It wouldn't be any good if it made the usual 'bleeping' noise – you'd get people reaching for their mobile phones as we walked through the train.

5	

Safety is the other important aspect of the job. If the train breaks down or is derailed, it's the conductor's job to protect the back of the train. The signalman will know where you are and warn the train behind to slow down, but we have to get out and walk down the track laying small packets of explosive. When the train behind goes over them, that's the signal to the driver to stop. It hasn't happened to me yet, but I'd know what to do if it did. At the moment I'm learning to be an operations trainer – training up new employees on the safety aspects of the railway.

6	

I'd wanted to be a conductor since I was a teenager. I'd got to know the staff when I travelled on the trains to school and it seemed like interesting work. I left school at 16 and started a training scheme the same year. My first position was as an office messenger, but I soon moved on to working on the trains.

7	

At the end of the day I sign off and hand over the ticket machine and any money I've collected selling tickets. I like the travelling side of the job and meeting people. We get to know the regular passengers quite well and a friendly comment can make your day really happy.

Part 2

You are going to read a newspaper article about someone who collects dolls. For
Questions **8–14**, choose the answer (**A, B, C** or **D**) which you think fits best according to
the text.
Mark your answers **on the separate answer sheet**.

The doll collector

'This is the real star of the collection,' says
Cynthia Lole, wide eyes shining, holding up a 12
cm-high pink plastic doll to my face. It looks
much the same as the hundred or so other pink
plastic dolls arranged round the walls of her tiny
west London flat. But not to Cynthia. 'Look! It's
a boy!' she cries. 'I was so excited when I found
it.' All Cynthia's other dolls are girls. Not girls
in pretty dresses with blinking eyes and lots of
hair, though. She collects kewpie dolls – rubber
dolls with pointed heads and round faces that
have been manufactured in various countries
throughout the world for nearly a century.

Over the past five years or so she has gathered
together big ones and little ones, sitting-up ones
and lying-down ones, crying kewpies, crawling
kewpies, kewpies sucking their thumbs. There's
a large 1930s kewpie, a rare black kewpie with
no eyes, key-ring kewpies from Japan, a kewpie
box whose head lifts off as the lid. 'They've all
got slightly different expressions because they
are of different ages and come from different
countries,' she explains. 'This one's sweet, isn't
she? She's Italian,' she says picking up a
particularly attractive example with a cute smile
and a round stomach.

In every shade of pink from strawberry ice-
cream to flesh, the dolls form a six-deep guard
on wall shelves in Cynthia Lole's spare
bedroom. Ninety pairs of painted eyes seem to
turn on you as you pass the door – they're not
exactly threatening, but Cynthia says she's had
business visitors drop their briefcases open-
mouthed at the sight of them. The rarest
examples are behind glass in the bathroom – tiny
kewpies no more than four centimetres high
from the 1920s. The very earliest ones were
made from porcelain, but Cynthia's collection
doesn't go back that far: 'It's a fun thing, so I

don't want to spend big money. Most of these
cost very little, although I did pay rather more for
the boy.'

As with most collections, Cynthia's started
with just one: a very ordinary example she
bought in a local London market. 'Then I found a
few more, and before I knew it, the dealers were
saving them for me and people were buying me
them as presents.' She had about 25 or so before
she became a serious collector. 'I brought home
this bright pink light from a film I'd been
working on, and when I put it on in the bedroom,
all the kewpies' eyes lit up and their heads started
glowing. I thought – yeah! – I'm going to have a
whole shelf of them with a light behind.'

Now Cynthia hunts down kewpies wherever
she goes, from local street markets and specialist
doll dealers to work trips abroad, from
Philadelphia to Portugal, with her job making
pop videos. Quick as a flash, she can remember
the origin of each: 'That one I found in New York
just as I was leaving to catch a plane. There it was
for only a dollar. And that dear little one in the
red suit a friend found in San Francisco.'

Kewpie dolls are the most recent of Cynthia's
addictions, but the flat is a monument to a
lifetime of collecting. She began in her
childhood, probably as a reaction against her
parents, who hated having lots of unnecessary
things around and would say things like: 'Why
do you need another vase if you've already got
one?'

In the early days it was just cardboard boxes,
but she started collecting seriously when she
moved to London to work and discovered the
street markets. One of her interests is old
advertising signs and she also collects things
from the videos she has worked on – a model
1950s plane hangs from the ceiling and there is a
rubber octopus on the television. 1960s pop
music plays on a 1954 jukebox machine that had

to be brought in through the window when Cynthia moved here six years ago – she'd got the measurements of the hall wrong and they even had to remove the window frame. 'Being such an enthusiastic collector does have its drawbacks,' she sighs. 'It's not only moving house – I've been warned I could never have a cleaner because it would take them hours just to dust and as for the dolls, they'd probably take one look and resign on the spot.'

8   What is the writer's first impression of Cynthia's dolls?
   A   They are mostly girls.
   B   They all look very similar.
   C   They have a lot of hair.
   D   They are very old.

9   What does the writer learn from Cynthia about kewpie dolls?
   A   They were originally children's toys.
   B   Their faces differ in detail.
   C   The best ones come from Italy.
   D   Older examples are often damaged.

10   How does Cynthia display most of her dolls?
   A   She protects them from visitors.
   B   She keeps frightening ones by the door.
   C   She has a glass case in her bedroom.
   D   She displays them all around her flat.

11   How did Cynthia begin collecting dolls?
   A   She bought a boy doll in London.
   B   She started with porcelain dolls.
   C   She found a doll in a market.
   D   She was given a doll as a present.

12   When did Cynthia become a serious doll collector?
   A   when she saw how the dolls looked lit up
   B   when she started working on pop videos
   C   when she began travelling on business
   D   when she found a specialist doll dealer

13   How did Cynthia's background influence her choice of hobby?
   A   Her parents gave her dolls.
   B   She started collecting vases.
   C   Her family discouraged collecting.
   D   She was surrounded by unnecessary objects.

14   What problems do Cynthia's collections cause?
   A   Moving around her flat is difficult.
   B   The cleaner has threatened to resign.
   C   There is not room to display everything.
   D   She has problems when she moves house.

Part 3

You are going to read an article about an underwater museum. Seven sentences have been removed from the article. Choose from the sentences **A–H** the one which fits each gap (**15–20**). There is one extra sentence which you do not need to use. There is an example at the beginning (**0**).

Mark your answers **on the separate answer sheet**.

Underwater World

If you want to dive in clear blue waters, find rich marine life and swim over the remains thrown away by ancient sailors, the tiny island of Ustica is the place to go. This island, 60km from the Italian coast, is the site of Europe's only underwater museum. **0** | *H* |

The clear waters attract some of the world's best underwater divers. The International Academy of Underwater Sciences, which was set up to encourage underwater exploration, is based in Ustica. **15** | |

Dr Honor Frost, a British underwater archaeologist and Golden Trident winner, believes that Ustica shows that some underwater remains are best left in the surroundings where they have been preserved for centuries. **16** | |

According to Frost, the establishment of the underwater museum has made an interesting area of sea floor, together with the objects which fell to it in antiquity, safe for future study. **17** [ ]

For example, it is puzzling that only iron anchors of quite a late date seem to have been lost there, despite local evidence of sea trade during a period nearly four thousand years ago, when stone anchors would have been in use. Among the anchors and other remains there are an extraordinary number of Roman millstones, which were widely traded throughout the ancient world. **18** [ ]

The charm of Ustica's underwater world, though, is not only in its historical objects. The sea of Ustica, as far as five kilometres from the coast, is considered to possess Italy's best underwater reserves, as well as some of the clearest waters in the Mediterranean. **19** [ ] You dive into a world of wonderful archaeological remains and fantastic colours: bright coral, an astonishing variety of seaweeds and colonies of sponges.

20 [ ] And since diving provides most of the island's income, the underwater archaeological park has been welcomed as an attraction which boatmen, guides and diving instructors offer to clients who have been drawn by the natural beauty to be found in the clear water of the island.

A Many questions remain to be answered about the museum site.

B Above these, within 15 metres of the surface, divers can see octopus and all kinds of fish.

C Made of volcanic rock, they were carried by corn ships heading from Rome to the ports of the north African coast.

D This excellent visibility – often up to 20 metres – makes it a great place for underwater photography.

E This gives divers the experience of underwater archaeology without disturbing important sites.

F However, this section of the museum, although already accessible to diving visitors, still contains material of interest to researchers.

G This month it presented its Golden Trident awards, the underwater equivalent of the Nobel prizes, which have been awarded annually since 1960.

H Only here can divers explore labelled exhibits such as anchors, pots and millstones, which fell to the sea floor centuries ago.

Part 4

You are going to read an article about different kinds of rice. For Questions **21–35**, choose from the kinds of rice (**A–I**). Some kinds may be chosen more than once. When more than one answer is required, these may be given in any order. There is an example at the beginning (**0**).

Mark your answers **on the separate answer sheet**.

According to the writer which rice ...

is creamy when cooked?	**0**	*A*
needs continual attention while cooking?	**21**	
suits the method of eating it?	**22**	
is often served with another kind?	**23**	
can be served sweetened?	**24**	**25**
comes in two colours?	**26**	**27**
is related to rice introduced from another country?	**28**	
is unpopular in some parts of the world?	**29**	
has grains which do not stick together when cooked?	**30**	
requires two different cooking processes?	**31**	
is found wherever rice is grown?	**32**	

is too dry for some dishes?

| 33 | |

is best cooked over a long period of time?

| 34 | | | 35 | |

The World of Rice

More than half of all the food eaten in the world is rice and there are hundreds of varieties. ROSEMARY STARK looks at the main varieties and which dishes they are best suited for.

European   A

Of the European varieties, Arborio is the favourite for risotto, the popular Italian rice dish. Its grains take up plenty of meat juices to cook to soft creaminess. A risotto should be served very moist, and constant stirring is required as you add liquid to ensure this.

Basmati   B

One of the most famous eastern rices is Basmati. Thin and long-grained, it grows in the foothills of the Himalayas, where its name means 'fragrant'. You can find a brownish black version as well as the more familiar snowy white grain used to accompany the hot spicy dishes of the region. Cook it for eight minutes in plenty of boiling salted water, drain, then continue cooking with butter in a tightly covered pan for a further 10–15 minutes over a very low heat.

Patna   C

Patna rice, long-grained and fragrant, is good-tempered in cooking because it

keeps a firm centre while the grains stay separate. Grown in north India, it is good for rice salads and makes a fine accompaniment to Indian food.

Thai   D

Thai Fragrant or Jasmine rice is young and tender, long-grained, slightly sticky and wonderfully scented. Good hot or in cold rice salads, it is a southeast Asian favourite.   ⟫→

Glutinous — E

Glutinous rice comes in fairly short grains, black or white. Its stickiness makes it popular where food is eaten using chopsticks. In China and Japan it is also flavoured with sugar and served with raw fish.

Java — F

Java, a short-grained variety, is good in slow-baked dishes, particularly rice puddings. Eighty grams of rice with three hours of the gentlest baking can take up at least a litre of milk and sugar, swelling to a softness under a thick golden skin.

Carolina — G

Rice is an important crop in the US too. Carolina rice is descended from seed brought from Italy by Thomas Jefferson, but the modern variety is not a good risotto rice: its longer grains swell well in cooking but to a drier finish than risotto-makers would want.

Wild — H

Wild rice, from North America, is not strictly a rice, but the shiny long black seed of a wild grass. Something of a luxury, it is handsome mixed with white rice. Since wild rice takes up almost twice as much water in cooking as white rices, a little goes a long way.

Brown — I

Brown rice, the grain in its natural state, is to be found in all rice-growing districts, but depends for its modern popularity on the fashion for unprocessed food in America and parts of Europe. The outer layer gives it a nutty flavour, but it needs more cooking than white varieties. It is eaten less in those areas where rice is a normal part of the daily diet.

PAPER 2   WRITING (1 hour 30 minutes)

Part 1

You **must** answer this question.

1   You have a friend who lives in another country and you receive a letter from him/her inviting you to stay. You have never been to his/her country before and you are very excited about the invitation.

Part of the letter is printed below. Read it carefully and write a reply accepting the invitation. Tell your friend what you would be interested in doing and ask for some information to help you plan your trip, using the notes that you have made. You may add relevant ideas of your own.

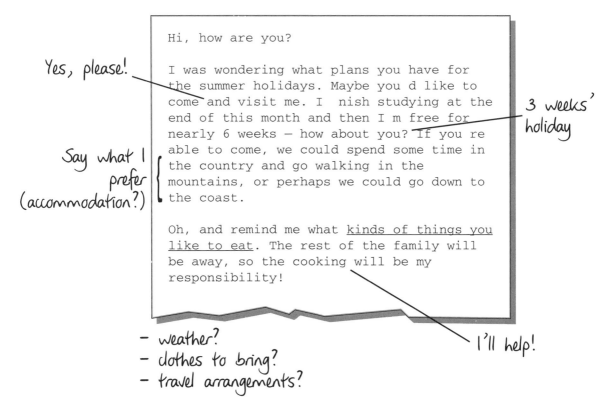

Yes, please!

Say what I prefer (accommodation?)

> Hi, how are you?
>
> I was wondering what plans you have for the summer holidays. Maybe you d like to come and visit me. I nish studying at the end of this month and then I m free for nearly 6 weeks — how about you? If you re able to come, we could spend some time in the country and go walking in the mountains, or perhaps we could go down to the coast.
>
> Oh, and remind me what kinds of things you like to eat. The rest of the family will be away, so the cooking will be my responsibility!

3 weeks' holiday

I'll help!

- weather?
- clothes to bring?
- travel arrangements?

Write **a letter** of between **120** and **180** words in an appropriate style on the next page. Do not write any addresses.

Part 1

....
....
....
....
....
....
....
....
....
....
....
....
....
....
....
....
....
....
....
....
....
....
....
....
....
....
....

Part 2

Write an answer to **one** of the questions **2–5** in this part. Write your answer in **120–180** words in an appropriate style on the next page. Put the question number in the box.

2   You have recently been involved in a class activity listening to interviews with famous sports personalities. Your teacher has now asked you to write a composition, giving your views on the following statement:

Famous sports people earn far too much money nowadays.

Write your **composition**.

3   You have seen the following announcement in an international young people's magazine:

You are what you wear!

Are clothes important to you and your friends?
Is there really a connection between clothes and personality?

We invite readers to write and tell us what their views are on the subject.
We will publish the three most interesting articles.

Write your **article**.

4   You are a member of an International Film Club and recently helped to organise a Film Festival in your area. Now you have been asked to write a report on the festival for the Club committee, covering the problems as well as the successes.

Write your **report**.

5   **Background reading texts**

Answer **one** of the following two questions based on your reading of **one** of the set books.

(a) Your teacher has asked you to write a composition explaining how you think a new character could be added to the book or one of the short stories you have read. Write your **composition**, explaining what type of character you would add and saying how your character would change the story.

(b) Does the front cover of the book you have read succeed in making the book look interesting to someone who has not yet read it? Write a **composition**, describing the front cover and explaining how it relates to the book.

Part 2

Question	

....
....
....
....
....
....
....
....
....
....
....
....
....
....
....
....
....
....
....
....
....
....
....
....
....
....
....

PAPER 3   USE OF ENGLISH (1 hour 15 minutes)

Part 1

For Questions **1–15**, read the text below and decide which answer, **A**, **B**, **C** or **D** best fits each space. There is an example at the beginning (**0**).
Mark your answers **on the separate answer sheet**.

Example:

0   A early   **B** starting   **C** beginning   **D** original

0	A	B	C	D
	▄	▁	▁	▁

FILM MUSIC

In the **(0)** .... days of the cinema, before sound was introduced, silent films were **(1)** .... by a pianist, or even a small orchestra playing in the cinema itself. One reason for this was to **(2)** .... up the noise of the projector. However, a more important role was to provide **(3)** .... for what was going on in the film, and **(4)** .... the audience through the story. Different kinds of music were **(5)** .... with different situations, such as fights, chases, romantic scenes and so on. Music was also used to identify the geographical location or historical setting of the story. In **(6)** ...., individual characters often had their own tune, which could also **(7)** .... what sort of person they were.

Music **(8)** .... something extra to what was happening on the flat screen. It could create atmosphere and **(9)** .... the involvement of the audience, one moment encouraging them to relax, the next developing a **(10)** .... of tension. And all this was done without any words being spoken.

Audiences at that **(11)** .... would have been **(12)** .... with the musical language connected with the traditions of popular theatre, and many of these were **(13)** .... to the new medium of the cinema. Today, **(14)** .... the films produced may be technically very different from before, much of the musical history still **(15)** .....

1	**A**	chased	**B**	pursued	**C**	taken	**D**	accompanied
2	**A**	tie	**B**	put	**C**	cover	**D**	make
3	**A**	support	**B**	description	**C**	suggestion	**D**	comment
4	**A**	persuade	**B**	guide	**C**	follow	**D**	send
5	**A**	associated	**B**	united	**C**	joined	**D**	collected
6	**A**	measure	**B**	addition	**C**	plus	**D**	total
7	**A**	point	**B**	indicate	**C**	paint	**D**	draw
8	**A**	placed	**B**	made	**C**	added	**D**	put
9	**A**	increase	**B**	rise	**C**	grow	**D**	lift
10	**A**	look	**B**	meaning	**C**	sight	**D**	sense
11	**A**	time	**B**	spell	**C**	occasion	**D**	century
12	**A**	popular	**B**	educated	**C**	familiar	**D**	experienced
13	**A**	transferred	**B**	moved	**C**	transported	**D**	carried
14	**A**	instead	**B**	however	**C**	despite	**D**	although
15	**A**	remains	**B**	stays	**C**	keeps	**D**	rests

Part 2

For Questions **16–30**, read the text below and think of the word which best fits each space. Use only **one** word in each space. There is an example at the beginning (**0**). Write your answers **on the separate answer sheet**.

Example: | **0** | *another* |

LEARNING BODY LANGUAGE

Throughout history people have always communicated with one (**0**) ...., not only by speech but also by movements of the hands and body. It is, however, only (**16**) .... the last few years that these aspects of communication (**17**) .... been studied at all widely. This type of communication is (**18**) .... as body language or non-verbal communication.

People sometimes wonder (**19**) .... you can learn how body language works. It is of course possible to read books on the subject but you also need to (**20**) .... time observing people's movements. A railway station is a particularly good place (**21**) .... such observation, as here people can (**22**) .... seen openly expressing eagerness, sorrow, delight, impatience and many other human emotions by means of movement.

If you turn down the sound on your television set and try to understand (**23**) .... is happening simply by watching (**24**) .... picture you will learn even more about communication (**25**) .... words. By turning the sound back up every five minutes (**26**) .... so, it is possible to check (**27**) .... accurate your understanding is.

Having studied the art of body language you will have (**28**) .... definite advantage at a boring party. You will be able to sit on your own for the whole evening and thoroughly enjoy (**29**) .... by both watching (**30**) .... interpreting the body language of all the other people there.

Part 3

For Questions **31–40**, complete the second sentence so that it has a similar meaning to the first sentence, using the word given. **Do not change the word given.** You must use between two and five words, including the word given. There is an example at the beginning (**0**).
Write **only** the missing words **on the separate answer sheet**.

Example:

0   My brother is too young to drive a car.
   not

   My brother .... drive a car.

The gap can be filled by the words 'is not old enough to' so you write:

0	*is not old enough to*

---

31   She did not buy the car because it was too expensive.
   it

   She would have bought the car .... so expensive.

32   He managed to make some extra money by writing stories.
   order

   He wrote stories .... make some extra money.

33   My father thinks that people who watch television are wasting their time.
   a

   My father thinks watching television .... people's time.

34   You won't have to go to the meeting next week.
   necessary

   It will .... to go to the meeting next week.

35   My friend had not expected the film to be so funny.
   friend

   The film .... had expected.

36 Martin has to wear his glasses to read the newspaper.
without

Martin .... wearing his glasses.

37 Alan's children are never invited to parties now because of their bad behaviour.
that

Alan's children .... they are never invited to parties.

38 It was fortunate for him that he wasn't injured in the accident.
lucky

He .... be injured in the accident.

39 Carole is the only person I know who enjoys homework.
apart

I don't know .... Carole who enjoys homework.

40 I did not think that Peter would phone tonight.
unlikely

I .... to phone tonight.

Part 4

For Questions **41–55**, read the text and look carefully at each line. Some of the lines are correct, and some have a word which should not be there.

If a line is correct, put a tick (✓) by the number **on the separate answer sheet**. If a line has a word that should **not** be there, write the word **on the separate answer sheet**. There are two examples at the beginning (**0** and **00**).

Examples:

0	*of*

00	✓

A DAY OUT

0	For the last few of months I have spent every Saturday in my flat and
00	have done nothing more exciting than work at home, read the
41	newspaper and watch television. I had begun feeling bored with this
42	and so, last weekend I thought I would do something different. I
43	rang up several of my other friends and we decided to go to London
44	for the day. I was really excited as I hadn't never been to London
45	since I was ten years. We decided to go by coach as this was by far
46	the most cheapest means of transport that was available even though
47	it meant that we needed to get up very early. Once in London we
48	decided to take on a sightseeing tour as we wanted to see some of the
49	famous buildings. After the tour we bought some sandwiches and
50	ate them in a too small park. In the afternoon two of us went
51	shopping and the others went to the theatre. We met up
52	again at 6.30 p.m. and went to eat a small restaurant in Soho. The meal
53	was really good but, unfortunately, it took much longer time than we
54	had been expected. We had to get a taxi back to the coach station.
55	Luckily, we got there just two minutes before that our coach left.

Part 5

For Questions **56–65**, read the text below. Use the word given in capitals at the end of each line to form a word that fits in the space in the same line. There is an example at the beginning (**0**).

Write your answers **on the separate answer sheet.**

Example: | **0** | *interesting* |

AN EXHIBITION

People wishing to spend an **(0)** .... couple of hours in Railey this	**INTEREST**
month should visit the Town Hall where an exhibition of fifty **(56)**	**PAINT**
by the locally born **(57)** .... John Wragg is being held. The exhibition	**ART**
contains many extremely **(58)** .... pictures of Australia where John	**IMPRESS**
has lived for the past thirty years. However, he still has many **(59)**	**CONNECT**
with the **(60)** .... area as several members of his family live in Railey.	**SURROUND**
John hoped to be present for the official **(61)** .... of the exhibition but	**OPEN**
(62) .... he has been prevented from travelling to England because of	**FORTUNATE**
(63)	**ILL**
The exhibition is open **(64)** .... until the end of the month. The price of	**DAY**
(65) .... is £3 for adults and £2 for senior citizens, students and	**ADMIT**
children.	

PAPER 4 LISTENING (approximately 40 minutes)

Part 1

You will hear people talking in eight different situations. For Questions **1–8**, choose the best answer **A**, **B** or **C**.

---

1 Listen to this man talking to his friend about a meeting.
  Who turned up at the meeting?

A	Marian	1
B	James	
C	Alison	

2 You hear a man complaining about the place where he works.
  What is the problem in the office?

A	the heat	2
B	the noise	
C	the pollution	

3 You hear somebody talking about choosing a name for something.
  What is he talking about?

A	a children's toy	3
B	a computer game	
C	a rock band	

4 You hear somebody talking about the sport of badminton.
  What point is she making about the sport?

A	It's very popular.	4
B	It can be dangerous.	
C	It's quite exciting.	

5 A friend tells you about the time he was robbed.
What was his feeling about the incident?

   A   He felt surprised.

   B   He felt angry.

   C   He felt lucky.

	5

6 You hear the beginning of a radio programme.
What is the programme going to be about?

   A   farming

   B   baking

   C   building

	6

7 Listen to this man talking on the radio.
Who is he?

   A   an ambulance driver

   B   a weatherman

   C   a policeman

	7

8 Listen to this teacher talking about hiring bicycles.
Why is he speaking?

   A   to give a warning

   B   to change some plans

   C   to provide some directions

	8

Part 2

You will hear an interview with a woman called Diana Walton at the old house which is her family home. For Questions **9–18**, complete each of the sentences.

Diana Walton's house

It is Britain's oldest house which was built as a [ ] **9**

In 1130, the front door was on [ ] **10**

The garden has a famous collection of [ ] **11**

People comment on the [ ] **12** in the garden.

Emily Watson was Diana's [ ] **13**

Emily's first book was called [ ] **14**

Emily's son, Peter, [ ] **15** in the book.

Some people who visit the house

recognise [ ] **16** described in the book.

People like the house because it has a feeling of [ ] **17**

The house also has a famous collection of [ ] **18**

Part 3

You will hear five different men talking about silence. For Questions **19–23**, choose from the list **A–F** who is speaking. Use the letters only once. There is one extra letter which you do not need to use.

A   a lawyer

B   a teacher

C   an actor

D   a sportsman

E   a disc jockey

F   a TV interviewer

Speaker 1   **19**

Speaker 2   **20**

Speaker 3   **21**

Speaker 4   **22**

Speaker 5   **23**

Part 4

You will hear a conversation between three people who are organising a sports day in their village. For Questions **24–30**, write **S** for **Susan**, **A** for **Alan** or **M** for **Marie**.

---

24 Who makes a recommendation? ☐ 24

25 Who offers to do something? ☐ 25

26 Who gives some advice? ☐ 26

27 Who refuses to accept an explanation? ☐ 27

28 Who makes a promise? ☐ 28

29 Who disagrees with a proposal? ☐ 29

30 Who has already got some information? ☐ 30

PAPER 5   SPEAKING (approximately 14 minutes)

You take the Speaking test with another candidate, referred to here as your partner. There are two examiners. One will speak to you and your partner and the other will just be listening. Both examiners will award marks.

Part 1 (3 minutes)

The examiner asks you and your partner questions about yourselves. You may be asked about things like 'your home town', 'your interests', 'your career plans', etc.

Part 2 (4 minutes)

The examiner gives you two photographs and asks you to talk about them for about one minute. The examiner then asks your partner a question about your photographs and your partner responds briefly.

Then the examiner gives your partner two different photographs. Your partner talks about these photographs for about one minute. This time the examiner asks you a question about your partner's photographs and you respond briefly.

Part 3 (3 minutes)

The examiner asks you and your partner to talk together. You may be asked to discuss something, solve a problem or perhaps come to a decision about something. For example, you might be asked to decide the best way to use some rooms in a language school. The examiner gives you a picture to help you but does not join in the conversation.

Part 4 (4 minutes)

The examiner joins in the conversation. You all talk together in a more general way about what has been said in Part 3. The examiner asks you questions but you and your partner are also expected to develop the conversation.

SAMPLE ANSWER SHEETS

CAMBRIDGE
EXAMINATIONS, CERTIFICATES AND DIPLOMAS
ENGLISH AS A FOREIGN LANGUAGE

University of Cambridge
Local Examinations Syndicate
International Examinations

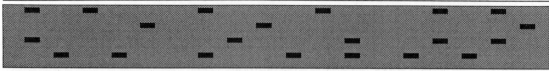

Examination Details	9999/01	99/D99
Examination Title	First Certificate in English	
Centre/Candidate No.	AA999/9999	
Candidate Name	A.N. EXAMPLE	

For Supervisor's use only

Shade here if the candidate is
ABSENT or has WITHDRAWN

• Sign here if the details above are correct

• Tell the Supervisor now if the details above
  are not correct

X

Candidate Answer Sheet: FCE Paper 1 Reading

Use a pencil

Mark ONE letter for each
question.

For example, if you think **B** is
the right answer to the
question, mark your answer
sheet like this:

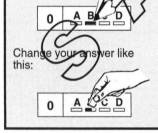

| 0 | A B C D |

Change your answer like
this:

| 0 | A B C D |

1	A B C D E F G H I
2	A B C D E F G H I
3	A B C D E F G H I
4	A B C D E F G H I
5	A B C D E F G H I

6	A B C D E F G H I
7	A B C D E F G H I
8	A B C D E F G H I
9	A B C D E F G H I
10	A B C D E F G H I
11	A B C D E F G H I
12	A B C D E F G H I
13	A B C D E F G H I
14	A B C D E F G H I
15	A B C D E F G H I
16	A B C D E F G H I
17	A B C D E F G H I
18	A B C D E F G H I
19	A B C D E F G H I
20	A B C D E F G H I

21	A B C D E F G H I
22	A B C D E F G H I
23	A B C D E F G H I
24	A B C D E F G H I
25	A B C D E F G H I
26	A B C D E F G H I
27	A B C D E F G H I
28	A B C D E F G H I
29	A B C D E F G H I
30	A B C D E F G H I
31	A B C D E F G H I
32	A B C D E F G H I
33	A B C D E F G H I
34	A B C D E F G H I
35	A B C D E F G H I

CAMBRIDGE
EXAMINATIONS, CERTIFICATES AND DIPLOMAS
ENGLISH AS A FOREIGN LANGUAGE

University of Cambridge
Local Examinations Syndicate
International Examinations

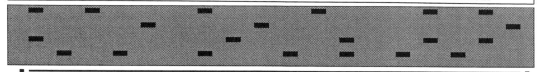

For Supervisor's use only

Shade here if the candidate is
ABSENT or has WITHDRAWN

➡ ▭ ⬅

Examination Details	9999/03	99/D99
Examination Title	First Certificate in English	
Centre/Candidate No.	AA999/9999	
Candidate Name	A.N. EXAMPLE	

• Sign here if the details above are correct

⊠

- -
• Tell the Supervisor now if the details above
are not correct

Candidate Answer Sheet: FCE Paper 3 Use of English

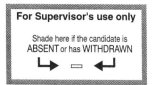

Use a pencil

For **Part 1**: Mark ONE letter for each question.

For example, if you think **C** is the
right answer to the question,
mark your answer sheet like this:

0	A̲ B̲ C̲ D̲

For **Parts 2, 3, 4** and **5**: Write your
answers in the spaces next to the
numbers like this:

0	example

Part 1				
1	A	B	C	D
2	A	B	C	D
3	A	B	C	D
4	A	B	C	D
5	A	B	C	D
6	A	B	C	D
7	A	B	C	D
8	A	B	C	D
9	A	B	C	D
10	A	B	C	D
11	A	B	C	D
12	A	B	C	D
13	A	B	C	D
14	A	B	C	D
15	A	B	C	D

Part 2	Do not write here
16	16
17	17
18	18
19	19
20	20
21	21
22	22
23	23
24	24
25	25
26	26
27	27
28	28
29	29
30	30

Turn
over
for
Parts
3 - 5
➡

Part 3		Do not write here		
31		31 0	1	2
32		32 0	1	2
33		33 0	1	2
34		34 0	1	2
35		35 0	1	2
36		36 0	1	2
37		37 0	1	2
38		38 0	1	2
39		39 0	1	2
40		40 0	1	2

Part 4	Do not write here
41	41
42	42
43	43
44	44
45	45
46	46
47	47
48	48
49	49
50	50
51	51
52	52
53	53
54	54
55	55

Part 5	Do not write here
56	56
57	57
58	58
59	59
60	60
61	61
62	62
63	63
64	64
65	65

110

CAMBRIDGE
EXAMINATIONS, CERTIFICATES AND DIPLOMAS
ENGLISH AS A FOREIGN LANGUAGE

University of Cambridge
Local Examinations Syndicate
International Examinations

For Supervisor's use only
Shade here if the candidate is ABSENT or has WITHDRAWN
➡ ▭ ⬅

Examination Details 9999/04 99/D99

Examination Title First Certificate in English

Centre/Candidate No. AA999/9999

Candidate Name A.N. EXAMPLE

• Sign here if the details above are correct

X

• Tell the Supervisor now if the details above are not correct

Candidate Answer Sheet: FCE Paper 4 Listening

Mark test version below
A B C D E

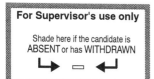

Use a pencil

For **Parts 1** and **3**:
Mark ONE letter for each question.

For example, if you think **B** is the right answer to the question, mark your answer sheet like this:

0	A	B	C

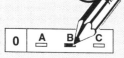

For **Parts 2** and **4**:
Write your answers in the spaces next to the numbers like this:

0	*example*

Part 1

1	A	B	C
2	A	B	C
3	A	B	C
4	A	B	C
5	A	B	C
6	A	B	C
7	A	B	C
8	A	B	C

Part 2		Do not write here
9		9
10		10
11		11
12		12
13		13
14		14
15		15
16		16
17		17
18		18

Part 3						
19	A	B	C	D	E	F
20	A	B	C	D	E	F
21	A	B	C	D	E	F
22	A	B	C	D	E	F
23	A	B	C	D	E	F

Part 4	Do not write here
24	24
25	25
26	26
27	27
28	28
29	29
30	30